The Far *Right*

Donald
Janson

& Bernard
Eismann

The
Far
Right

McGraw-Hill Book Company, Inc.
NEW YORK TORONTO LONDON

For Jane and Suzanne

Contents

Introduction

Global tensions, racial strife and other circumstances that have prompted the growth and activity of ultraconservative organizations today may ease tomorrow, dropping the Far Right at least temporarily out of the limelight. Yet the current surge of these groups, however unstable and erratic, is a phenomenon that has made an impact on the political and social life of the nation. It is a phenomenon that has occurred in related forms in the past and in all likelihood will recur in the future. Because of the changing nature and fleeting fortunes of many of the Right-wing organizations of today, this book does not attempt to draw a final picture of the Movement. It does seek to catch its image and assess its importance.

In compiling this report, we traveled to most of the states of the Union and spoke with or listened to most of the leaders of the Far Right. We attended meetings, both open and closed, of the principal organizations of the Movement, and read much of the swelling output of "Americanist" literature. Where neither of us was able to go, we enlisted the help of informed persons on the scene.

The report is on the Far Right, and distinguishes throughout between this extremist element and the responsible conservatism represented by Right-wing spokesmen of the major
political parties in the United States and others. Although
the views of the Far Right and the "responsible" Right frequently coincide or overlap, the two groups differ in their
approaches to achieving their aims. Only the Far Rightist
attributes pro-Communist motivation to all who disagree
with him.

We are grateful to radio, television, wire-service, newspaper, and magazine reporters throughout the country who
helped us keep closely in touch with the fluid situation on
the Far Right. We thank them and their companies and publications. We also thank the historians, sociologists, psycholo-
gists, educators, politicians, and others who contributed time
and resources.   *Donald Janson and Bernard Eismann*

one:
The Movement

1:
Right Face!

The winter night on Chicago's North Side is peaceful. The lazily swirling snow forms a halo around the globes of the glowing street lamps.

A young man, barely past his teens, hunches his shoulders into a short black jacket and bows his head to keep the flakes from his face. His long hair is plastered back at the sides and partly covered with feathers of snow. Now and then he passes through the yellow light that sifts through the picture windows of well-kept but old asbestos-shingled houses.

Others come down the same street. A heavy middle-aged woman, her high-collared coat pulled tight around her, advances with uncertain steps. A tall man with black hair and mustache, his lanky frame hidden by a heavy tweed overcoat, walks with assurance; he shakes his head now and then to keep the snow from his thick-lens glasses.

And there are a few more, all bound for the same place. They trudge through a narrow alley to the rear of an old frame house and climb the wooden steps to an attic apartment. A door opens. Soon, boots and coats off and put away, they sit down.

3

Nine men and two women, one with a child in her arms, gather in the tiny living room. A toddler roams about looking at the guests. As she is taken to bed, she clutches a pamphlet with the headline RED INFILTRATION AT THE PENTAGON. The sticker on an envelope in her other hand proclaims in blue italic print: *This is a Republic, not a Democracy—Let's keep it that way.*

The eleven members of this chapter of the John Birch Society settle down for their meeting; they have the word for the month directly from headquarters—from the pen of the Founder, Robert Henry Winborne Welch, Jr.

A dusty one-lane gravel road winds deep into the wooded Bostons, an imposing escarpment in the Arkansas Ozarks. There is no sign of life for miles of treacherous second-gear driving. The rocky trail finally ends in a clearing that discloses a weatherbeaten home, an automobile, and a brace of razorbacks.

The owners, lately of California, greet the visitors pleasantly, offer them pawpaws, and converse readily. It doesn't take them long to explain that the remote reaches of the hills are becoming a haven for "conservatives" concerned about the possibility of Communist assault and takeover of the nation. The host quotes a fellow ex-Californian in another Ozark retreat as saying "God have mercy on my carefree friends on the Coast if the Reds—and there are hordes of them out there—take us over from within or blast us from the outside."

The high grass near the banks of the Missouri River in rural Missouri rustles as a handful of men in military fatigues crawl through on their bellies. Some carry automatic rifles, one packs a trench mortar on his back, another pulls a field radio. They stop when they see the river and their leader scans the water through his glasses. He reports he has sighted the Russian gunboat.

These are Minutemen, American citizens training themselves to fight as armed guerrillas once the enemy has taken over.

Many others see the peril. Young naval officers taking leadership training in San Diego are told by their petty-officer instructor that there are card-carrying Communists in high places in the country. A crewman aboard the USS *Randolph* boasts to a newsman that there is an active Birch Chapter on the carrier. A California congressman lists his membership in the John Birch Society as the first entry next to his name in the *Congressional Directory*. A Long Island housewife warns her neighbors that local suppliers are selling Russian peatmoss.

An Australian preacher, a Dallas garageman, a Texas rancher, a Tulsa evangelist, a covey of ex-FBI men and retired military officers—superpatriots of every stripe are beating the same anvil:

The enemy is within. We are the victims of subversives at home. The real threat to America is not from Russia but from secret agents of the Communist conspiracy here—your garden-supply dealer, the high school principal, the superintendent of the town waterworks, your congressman.

The alarms are broadcast from a thousand platforms, in several million pamphlets, brochures, and booklets. They are echoed at town meetings, in letters to congressmen, in high school auditoriums, at anti-Communist seminars, in living rooms.

Suspicion spreads until it creates a crisis in a state or county political organization, puts a parade of pickets outside the White House, the United Nations, Madison Square Garden, a local library. Sometimes it gets out of hand—a bundle of dynamite, some tape and then, in the night, an explosion. The homes of two California ministers who spoke out against the pronouncements of the Far Right are shattered.

The wave of Right-wing extremism took form during

Dwight D. Eisenhower's presidency, but it had no real strength then. Its spokesmen clattered along in the trough of discredited McCarthyism, haranguing skimpy meetings with outbursts of frustration that stemmed from setbacks in the cold war, the impossibility of America's isolation from world troubles, and the spreading briar patch of domestic bureaucracy and taxation. The presence of a benign and popular General of the Army in the White House had a calming influence on people and kept the Rightists' audiences small.

The Movement accelerated when President Eisenhower was on his way out. Neither nominee to succeed him was satisfactory to the ultraconservatives. Campaign talk of a missile gap fed their frustration. Berlin nurtured it. So did Laos. John F. Kennedy's election buttressed their worst fears.

Many of the frustrated and anxious became converts to Birchism, with its simple solutions to complex problems. Pamphleteers turned to with renewed will. The plotting hand of communism received credit for every disappointing turn on the local, national, and world scene, shaking the confidence of the credulous.

The Bay of Pigs fiasco broke the dike. President Kennedy was pilloried by the superpatriots as a "no-win" chief. The stalemate in Vietnam and the Congo imbroglio heightened vexation. More and more citizens became concerned, and the Far Right capitalized on their worries. The well-organized Birch Society enrolled thousands of dues-paying members—military men, businessmen, professors, legislators, and clergymen among them. Moneyed industrialists were key converts.

The Far Right became a fount of proposals born of frustration and put forward in the name of anticommunism. Slick promotion drew crowd after crowd to hear the message. Twelve thousand persons filled the Hollywood Bowl for a glittering production, and hundreds of other programs were staged throughout the land. Meetings ranged from vast to intimate, sober to bizarre. Extremist preachers mixed religion with politics and drew crowds to revival-like rallies, passing the hat in the name of the battle against atheistic communism.

First to produce a sizable following for the Far Right were the Southern and Southwestern bastions of religious fundamentalism and political conservatism and the upper-class suburbs of urban areas. Organizations, some no larger than neighborhood "study groups" with a few members, proliferated. Many were chapters or cells of national bodies. Over-all membership, in some cases secret and often disunited on issues, was estimated at more than a million by 1963.

The press lavished attention on the Movement. Newspapers, radio, magazines, and television reported the excesses of its leaders and criticized its antidemocratic direction. Robert Welch's characterization of General Eisenhower as a Communist agent was uncovered, printed, and deplored. Although "respectable" members of the Birch Society "dissociated" themselves from their leader's views on Eisenhower, they plugged ahead with Welch's work, and the organization continued to thrive.

Active-duty military commanders played host to anti-Communist seminars on their bases and attended or addressed Right-wing meetings elsewhere. Edwin A. Walker, Bircher major general who was relieved of his command after seeking to indoctrinate his troops with his philosophy, resigned from the Army and took up the cause on the hustings. Two Southern California congressmen revealed their Birch membership. Congressmen from the conservative coalition of both parties graced the speaker's platforms of Far Right affairs and consulted with spokesmen for the Ultra fringe in Washington. One letter-writing campaign followed another, and mail baskets in the national and state capitols filled with the output. Over the objections of some leading educators, some states passed bills outlining required high school courses on the merits of "Americanism" over communism. The heavy flow of scare letters influenced the legislative process in a number of states.

The nation's leaders, at first inclined to belittle the Birchers and their fellow travelers as pathetic political eccentrics, could no longer ignore the Right. Attorney General Robert F. Kennedy called them a source of "tremendous danger." President Kennedy took sharp note of "the discordant voice of extremism." General Eisenhower added that the United States needed no "superpatriots." Joining in the denunciation were Vice-President Lyndon Johnson, former Vice-President Richard Nixon, FBI Director J. Edgar Hoover, educators, and leaders of the Protestant, Catholic, and Jewish faiths.

But the Movement weathered each assault. It had never expected support from the nation's political leaders; it opposes most of them. It identifies as the enemy everyone with views anywhere to the left of those of Barry Goldwater. With both money and attention, the Movement has been able to exert a noticeable influence; Republicans have expressed special concern lest it damage their party by onus of association or by siphoning off votes and money.

Right-wing bookstores sprouted across the country to supply the demand for literature. Some corporations provided Rightist lectures and films for the edification of employees—on company time. Lights blazed late in living rooms as neighbors gathered to "study" the Communist peril.

The specific aims of today's Far Right are numerous enough to test the capacity of an electronic computer. Most reflect a yearning for earlier days when the ocean was a barrier to communication and enemy alike, and when government—small by today's standards—left more of everything, including income, to the individual.

In the glossary of the Far Right, foreign aid is immoral, a Communist plot to sap American resources; the United

Nations is a miserable Tower of Babel and a Communist spy center which the United States ought to leave; relations with the Soviet Union and its satellites should be severed post-haste, since any kind of accommodation is "impossible"; and a preventive war might be advisable "to stamp out the pestilence" (how such a war would be won without allies or "wasteful" defense spending is not explained).

While there is considerable cross-pollination among the groups on the fringe, not all agree on all points. Concerning the home front, however, there is a consensus that government is too pervasive and costly—as well as Communist-infiltrated—and that common sense and rugged Americanism have been largely siphoned off from its counsels. A random but limited list of subjects that hold particular interest for the archpatriots and how they feel about them, described in their own words, would look like this:

Collective bargaining—special privilege; abolish.
Union shop—travesty.
Civil liberties—cloak for subversion.
Social security—Communistic.
Integration—device to mongrelize the nation.
Freedom Riders—young punks.
Intellectuals—zombies posturing in a vacuum of their own
    creation.
Buying government bonds—unpatriotic.
Expanding role of federal government—parasitic.
Supreme Court—nest of Communists; impeach
    the Chief Justice.
State Department—heavily infiltrated; dupes.
Central Intelligence Agency—ditto.
Other federal government departments—ditto.
Federal aid to education—subversive.
Federal income tax—immoral; conspiracy to destroy free
    enterprise; abolish.

Picasso—ban Communist art.

Bolshoi Ballet in U.S.—cold-war tactical *coup* for the Reds.

City-manager form of government—Communist device.

National Council of Churches—Communist-infiltrated.

Harvard—ditto.

Several other universities—corrupt, employ mental prostitutes.

Textbooks not screened by the Right—likely to have immoral, liberal, or Communist slant.

Fluoridation of water—Communist plot to weaken nation's health.

Philanthropic foundations—suspect.

Urban renewal—Communist device to wipe out property rights.

Revised version of the Bible—Communist perversion of the Gospel.

Federal Reserve System—a mistake; abolish.

Democracy—deceptive; a fraud.

House Committee on Un-American Activities—solid Americans; allocate more funds.

The press—badly duped; boycott.

Berlin wall—tear down.

Cuba—invade.

Russia and her ilk—terminate recognition.

North Atlantic Treaty Organization—desert.

Signs borne outside the Hollywood Paladium as President Kennedy delivered a warning against "these counsels of fear and suspicion" provided another sampling:

No Jack for Jagan; General Walker for President; Where Is the Spirit of '76?; Clean Out the C.I.A.; We Are Not Afraid of Fallout—*We Are Afraid of Sellout; Veto Tito; Out with Adlai;* and *Chuck Chester.*

These are some of the sounds. They have a familiar ring— one that has also been heard in earlier periods of American history.

2:
Perspective

"You are to do what you are told and if you are asked about us you are to say 'I know nothing.'"

This is not the pledge demanded of a John Birch recruit in Mandan, North Dakota, or of a Minuteman in an oil-stained garage at Collinsville, Illinois. It is the general order given to new members of a secret political-action group formally organized at Shreveport, Louisiana, in 1841. From that pledge came the name by which one of the most danger-ous groups of political vandals ever to tramp across the American scene was known: the Know-Nothings.

The seeds of reaction are deep in the furrows of American history. They have flourished particularly in periods of na-tional crisis or widespread despair. Sometimes, as with the Know-Nothings in the 1850s, they bore a harvest of violence and fear.

During the first half of the nineteenth century, the Amer-ican-Republican Party, forerunner of the Know-Nothings, was horrified by the thought that Roman Catholics or

11

naturalized American citizens might obtain political equality in numbers that would match those of native-born Americans.

The new immigrants clustered together in the cities. Anti-Catholic riots erupted in Boston, Philadelphia, and New York. In the 1840s, the Know-Nothings became well enough organized to exert political influence. With the backing of the Whig Party, the Know-Nothings won control of New York City in 1844; in 1845 they carried Boston. They wanted naturalized citizens barred from holding public office and demanded that waiting time for American citizenship be extended to twenty-one years.

When the Whig Party withdrew its support, in 1847, the radicals were considered politically dead, but—as it turned out—they were merely dormant. The 1850s brought the greatest wave of immigration the United States had yet known. As the newcomers flooded ashore, suspicion of them increased. It turned from contempt into hatred and fear. By 1852, the Know-Nothings represented a widely prevalent shade of American public opinion that had to be recognized by every Democratic and Whig politician. Meeting secretly, local Know-Nothings selected the candidates and party they wanted to support. No public endorsements were made, but word of their choice was spread effectively.

Despite wide influence, the Know-Nothings lacked political organization and real leadership. When they entered national politics openly, in 1852, they were obliged to publish a platform. This spread dissension through the membership ranks and alienated some party supporters. Still, in 1854 Know-Nothing gains were remarkable. In four New England states the party elected governors or gained control of legislatures. They won offices in California, Kentucky, and Maryland, and came close to taking all major posts in six Southern states.

But this was the last gasp of the Know-Nothings as a major political force. The party was swamped in the 1856 election and its candidate, former President Millard Fillmore, roundly defeated. After the Civil War other anti-Catholic groups cropped up, such as the Order of the Little Red School House and the Get-There-America Benefit Association, but they lacked the potency of the old Know-Nothing Party.

By 1900 the United States was a nation of 76,000,000 people, more than 10,000,000 of them foreign-born. Know-Nothingism, which had more to feed on at the turn of the century than it had had fifty years earlier, did not reappear, but there was a new radicalism. Ultras of the Left were throwing bombs; strikers dynamited U.S. Steel. In the West, gunplay was the laborer's means of making himself heard.

Against this background the idea of a "Red menace" started to take hold in the American mind. By the end of World War I, *Marxism, Socialism, Red, Communist,* and *conspiracy* were commonplace words. And these terms, to a Western world shocked by the success of the Russian Revolution, began to denote everyday fears. Conservative Americans went on the defensive and the ignorant tended to panic in their fear of the invisible enemy.

President Woodrow Wilson's dying administration made little effort in national leadership toward the end, but showed almost religious zeal in hunting "radicals." In that pursuit the administration exerted the same force it had used against antiwar groups and "slackers" during the war years.

The challenge from Russia strongly influenced public attitude and action. Although the Wilson administration was not unfriendly to the newly established USSR, a "Red scare" was in full flood throughout the United States.

In 1919 Thomas Gregory, U.S. Attorney General, demanded that constitutional guarantees be suspended. He told patriotic organizations—the National Defense Society, the American Protective League, and others—to keep up their work of amateur spying on individuals or groups they considered subversive. The same year, with seven justices assenting and two (Holmes and Brandeis) dissenting, the

Supreme Court upheld a lower court's sedition conviction
of men and women who had distributed pamphlets that objected to American troops going to Siberia to "interfere" in
the Russian Revolution. Justice Holmes wrote the minority
opinion, in which he held that a man's expression of an un-
popular opinion did not create a "clear and present danger."

Discord continued. The rumblings from the Left were
even louder than those from the Right. A general strike that
paralyzed Seattle in 1919 was said to be the handiwork of
Moscow's agents. This was not true, except that the American Communist Party, then in its formative stages, issued
fiercely worded manifestos telling the strikers to overthrow
the government and follow the lead of the Bolsheviks. In
fact, the Communists had little contact with unions at that
time and were not involved in organizing the workers.

In the weeks before May Day 1919, riots broke out in one
American city after another. Bombs went through the mails
to Justice Holmes from the radicals of the Right and to
the new Attorney General, A. Mitchell Palmer, from the
radicals of the Left. In June a bomb went off in Palmer's
Washington home. Other explosions were heard around the
country. As a result, state after state passed sedition laws.
Some even banned public display of a red flag—any kind of
red flag—and others were urged to adopt press-censorship
laws. Mobs broke up labor meetings, and Socialists and
Wobblies (members of International Workers of the World)
were carried away and beaten. On Armistice Day 1919,
American Legionnaires marched in formation to IWW headquarters in Centralia, Washington, opened fire, and staged
a running gun battle. That night a crowd broke into the jail,
hauled out a Wobbly, and hanged him.

In New York state, the legislature's Lusk Committee had
agents in the field and nearly a thousand suspects were
rounded up in an "investigation" of Socialism. On November
7, 1919, Attorney General Palmer unleashed a series of raids

against radical groups. His agents brought in several hundred men and women, many of them members of the Union of Russian Workers, a predecessor of the Communist Party, U.S.A. In December the Justice Department deported 249 persons, all leaders of the Radical Left, on the SS *Buford,* a ship the newspapers called the "Soviet Ark." Later that month President Wilson went before Congress and supported his Attorney General's demand for federal legislation against peacetime acts of sedition. On the second day of January 1920, hundreds of federal agents raided union headquarters and Left-wing political groups' offices. Nearly 5000 men and women were arrested and held without respect for due process of law. Less than a week later five properly elected Socialist assemblymen were denied their seats in the New York state legislature. Legal process and constitutional rights were disregarded, and the anti-Reds began painting an image of themselves as something worse than what they were attempting to eradicate.

Sometime during that period's near-hysteria an emotional thermostat began to work. Public revulsion against beatings, bombings, and middle-of-the-night arrests was growing. It was more and more widely realized that the incidents of those frenzied years (1919 and 1920) were not evidence of any legitimate conservatism. The leading conservative thinkers of the day opposed the violation of civil liberties as much as the liberals did. The federal government, they charged, was more guilty of subverting American institutions than were the anarchists, Socialists, and Reds.

Finally, in the early spring of 1920, Justices Holmes and Hughes and Senator George W. Norris, among others, brought their political and personal influence to bear and the raids came to an end. Political deportations were stopped. The uproar ended as quickly as it had begun.

The despair, doubt, and cynicism of the Great Depression of the early 1930s reopened some of the wounds. To businessmen, to the upper classes, and to most people who voted against him, President Franklin D. Roosevelt became "that man." Conservatives considered him a traitor to his class and a corrupter of the Constitution. By the time the shock of his election had started to wear thin, they had organized to defeat him. To wage propaganda warfare against the New Deal, big business poured money into the National Association of Manufacturers and the United States Chamber of Commerce. The Liberty League, formed to muster support against the Roosevelt administration in the 1934 congressional election, became the political playground for the Reasonable Right of the time. Though the League's edges were frayed by radicals and haters, the organization sought to change government policy by persuasion and political action—as far as most businessmen would go. Few conservatives became involved in the emerging hate groups. There were wisps of smoke, though. General Smedley Butler told a congressional investigating committee that a group of Wall Street brokers had approached him in 1934 and asked if he would be willing to organize an armed revolt against the government. Even this was considered a minor matter; the projected *Putsch* turned out to be mostly talk.

The radicalism of the Right spawned in the Thirties was an odd mixture. It was economic and religious, it was native American and imported Fascist. Hate was the chief ingredient, and much of the hatred was directed toward Jews.

The pattern had already been set in Germany and Italy, and demagogues seemed to find in the rantings of Hitler and Mussolini the wave of the future. One organization after another was launched, each equipped with a duplicating machine and a mailing list. The bad times that had befallen America were the work of the "international bankers," the "interests," and the "foreigners." The machine of Capitalism had failed; instead of repairing it, the Ultras of the Right and Left wanted a new model.

Father Charles E. Coughlin was perhaps the most spectacular of the new breed. His radio audiences, sitting spellbound as he explained his prescription for "social justice," were estimated at 10,000,000. Broadcasts were peppered with anti-Semitism. In 1939 he formed his Christian Front.

It was a confusing period. For those who could not or would not think, there were easy ways to attain peace of mind. On the Left, the Communist Party made great strides in recruiting intellectuals. On the Right, the American Nazis preyed on the innate fears of a still-unsophisticated people. There were many choices to make. Should one join the Silver Shirts and swear allegiance to William Dudley Pelley or was the counsel of Father Coughlin enough? Could one believe in Gerald L. K. Smith and his cries for "economic justice"? Was Elizabeth Dilling right in saying that Marxist-banker-Jewish capitalists were responsible for everything? Could Dr. Francis Townsend's $200-a-month pension scheme really work?

By 1938 it was hard to tell who stood for what. Both ultra-Right and ultra-Left offered "economic security," dictatorship, and doctrine ready-made. Of course, neither appealed to most Americans. But there were significant holidays from sanity. Hitler's friend and unofficial ambassador to German-Americans, Fritz J. Kuhn, was organizing units of the *Amerikadeutscher Volksbund* in first-generation German communities across the country. Brown-shirted Bundists were *Heiling* and goose-stepping in summer camps in New Jersey and California and preaching at street corners in New York.

From the early days of World War II the Ultras of the Right virtually disappeared from sight. Even the Republican-led, isolationist America First Committee was wrecked by 1942. It had been formed in 1940 and would have left all of Europe to the Nazis.

Most Americans had little time for anyone who plumped

for fascism. In 1942 a ring of native Fascists that included Pelley was broken, its members prosecuted and jailed. In a variety of ways, some perfectly legal and others questionable, the vocal ultranationalist element was silenced.

The Ultras of the Left were not. The United States was allied with the Soviet Union; Communists and their sympathizers were ignored or tolerated. Throughout the Thirties and into the war and the postwar Forties, Communists and their agents had infiltrated sensitive government areas. Still, the first disclosures of Communist espionage at war's end did not throw the nation into a Red scare. There was nothing similar to the raids that marked the close of World War I. Exposure of Communist infiltration into United States government came in 1945 with the Amerasia case, producing great public surprise but limited outcry.

In 1946 the Atomic Energy Act specified that "the character, associations and loyalty" of employees be subject to FBI reports. Some scientists objected on grounds that neither the Atomic Energy Commission nor the FBI had the ability or the right to judge them as individuals. From this the controversy grew. On March 22, 1947, President Harry S. Truman ordered a federal investigation into the loyalty of every person working in sensitive branches of government.

Under the terms of this order, any "reasonable doubt" regarding loyalty was to be considered adequate grounds for dismissal from federal employment. "Reasonable doubt" included association with any one of ninety organizations, most of them Communist fronts, appearing on a Justice Department roster of organizations listed as subversive. If a man were fired he could appeal but his appeal, for the most part, meant little. He still was denied both access to the information that caused him to be fired and the right to face his accusers. In four years 212 government employees were fired as disloyal, 2000 quit rather than submit to investigation—many out of principle. More than 3,000,000 were cleared. There were great cries of alarm from liberals, but new evidences of Soviet spying were being unmasked regularly—the threat was real.

In 1948 eleven American Communists were brought to trial under the Smith Act of 1940. The act, denounced by liberals, called for the registration of aliens. Under it hundreds of Axis agents had been arrested and jailed and larger numbers deported during the war years.

But the Smith Act contained other clauses which had not been tested. They made it a crime to teach or advocate, or to join a group that taught or advocated, the forceful overthrow of the government. The test came in New York's Federal District Court when the first postwar cry of "witch hunt" was raised by the witches themselves. With Judge Harold Medina presiding, the eleven Communists came to trial. Between them and their lawyers they provided the court and the spectators a circus of shouting, immaterial objections, and hair-pulling tantrums. By the time they were convicted late in 1949, they had bankrupted themselves of any public sympathy. Soon after the conviction of the eleven, the Truman administration brought to trial in federal court dozens of lesser American Communist Party functionaries and obtained convictions.

In 1948 the House Committee on Un-American Activities heard Whittaker Chambers. Chambers, once a *Time* Magazine senior editor, had been a Soviet courier. He accused Alger Hiss, a onetime middle-level official in the Department of State, of having belonged to the Communist Party. Hiss sued Chambers for libel. Chambers supplied the committee copies of official documents he claimed Hiss had copied by typewriter and by hand. The committee, spearheaded by a new member, Representative Nixon of California, insisted on going deeper into the matter. It did. Public attention was riveted, and most of America could hardly believe the tales it was being told—the intrigue, the deception, the cleverness were things only a Communist could dream of. Hiss was indicted for perjury in denying to the House committee that he had passed secret documents to Chambers. In July 1948, a hung jury saved him, but in 1950 he was convicted and sentenced to five years in a federal penitentiary.

By then senators and congressmen were stumbling over one another in the rush to see who could get first and best recognition as a Red-hunter. By perseverance, guile, and gall, Senator Joseph R. McCarthy of Wisconsin was easily the winner. In Wheeling, West Virginia, on February 9, 1950, McCarthy waved a piece of paper before his audience at a meeting of the Women's Republican Club. On that paper, said McCarthy, was a list of 205 men in the State Department "known as Communists." The next day, in Salt Lake City, the charge remained the same but the numbers had changed. Now he said fifty-seven card-carrying members of the Communist Party were employed in the Department of State. McCarthy's charges were given top notice in the nation's newspapers and on radio and television. Many Americans, already appalled by exposure of Communists in government, were blinded.

The man and the ism that were McCarthy are part of recent American history, too fresh in mind to need detailed recounting. The excesses of the era seemed to ebb with the political death of the man. But as the 1950s passed, it became evident that a new threat had arisen. Now it was from a Russian orbiting in space and from stalemate at the diplomatic board. The result was again frustration, hurt pride, and genuine fear.

Public fear begets social illness. This time the illness had little of the anti-Catholicism of the Know-Nothings or the anti-Semitism of the Fascists. The Far Right of the early 1960s represented an antidemocratic illness, a curious blend of political unreality and religious evangelism mixed in some areas of the country with racial prejudice. It ascribed all the nation's problems to the nefarious influence of a network of traitors *within* the United States.

Preceding developments seemed to lend support to this view. Hiss had been jailed. Judith Coplon was convicted of giving information on American counterespionage methods to a Soviet agent. Klaus Fuchs walked into a British jail convicted of giving bomb secrets to the Russians, and his confessions gave the United States the leads that led to the conviction and jailing of Harry Gold and Morton Sobel and the execution of Julius and Ethel Rosenberg. The Rosenbergs were convicted of treason. Their crimes, experts testified, allowed the USSR to manufacture the nuclear bomb at least three or four years sooner than it could have otherwise.

Patriotic Americans were alarmed and conservatives who were discontented for other reasons provided a ready-made audience for the newest set of reckless radicals of the Right. For many the age of suspicion had been resurrected. Now it was time to ask "Is your neighbor a Red?"

two:
The Organizations

3:

The John Birch Society

February 3, 1962. At the tables beneath the red, white, and blue chandeliers of the Crystal Ballroom in the Schroeder Hotel, 600 Milwaukee diners turned expectantly toward the dais as the speaker was introduced. For many it was the first view of Robert Welch, the slight, white-haired man who had founded the John Birch Society in 1958 and was the country's most controversial conservative since Wisconsin's McCarthy.

After paying homage to the statesmanship of the late senator, Welch assured his listeners that despite what they might have gathered from advance notice in the press, he had no horns that were not retractable and his wife had forgotten to pack his brown shirt and black armbands. This sally, used with regularity in his speeches, turned out to be his only attempt at humor during the ninety-minute lecture on the evils of democracy.

Although the wiry little man spoke with warmth and conviction of "our once glorious Republic" and vigorously denounced the "Leftists" in government who had insidiously undermined it for the last fifty years, many of his listeners grew restless as he droned on, tracing the history of government from the time of Solon in Athens 2500 years ago. When he finally reached the punch line—"democracy is merely a deceptive phrase, a weapon of demagoguery and a perennial fraud"—he received an extended round of applause, one of the few of the evening.

Whether the audience was thrilled with the message or simply relieved that the colorless hour-and-a-half presentation had come to an end was not clear. But comments indicated a sense of disappointment that the Deliverer from the Communist conspiracy had turned out to be so ordinary-looking and so lacking in personal dynamism. "Why, he could be anybody's grandfather," one woman said.

Robert Welch was much more than that, as attested by the nationwide audience for his fulminations. To fill the shoes of his hero, the late Senator McCarthy, he dropped out of the family candy company in 1957, closing a twenty-year business career that had included seven years as a board member of the National Association of Manufacturers, service as a bank director, and his position as vice-president of the James O. Welch Candy Company of Cambridge, Massachusetts. He also gave up any further ambition to run for political office in Massachusetts, his home state, where he had unsuccessfully sought the Republican nomination for lieutenant governor in 1950.

The Number One Bircher was born in 1899 on a farm in North Carolina. His forebears were farmers and Southern Baptist preachers. Welch was graduated from the University of North Carolina at seventeen, spent a year at the Naval Academy, dropped out to be a writer, changed his mind, and completed two years at Harvard Law School. At each school his grades were good.

He was honored as "Candy Man of the Year" by his trade in 1947. After abandoning candy, anticommunism became his sole pursuit, often occupying sixteen hours a day of his time. Comparing the orderliness of a republic with the chaos of democracy is one objective of his writing and speeches. Another is to show that Communists, bent on misleading the unwary and subverting the government, may lurk anywhere, including the room in which Welch is speaking. His speeches make it clear that ever since Franklin D. Roosevelt there has been a steadily increasing campaign to convert the Founding Fathers' American Republic into a democracy to pave the way for takeover by the Communists.

The Birch organization has distributed leaflets citing a booklet "issued by the U.S. War Department Nov. 30, 1928" to prove that the Welch line is no mere gambit in semantics. The booklet is quoted as defining democracy as "a government of the masses" that "results in mobocracy . . . demagogism, license, agitation, discontent, anarchy." In a republic, on the other hand, "authority is derived through the election by the people of public officials best fitted to represent them," avoiding "the dangerous extreme of either tyranny or mobocracy" and resulting in "statesmanship, liberty, reason, justice, contentment and progress."

The leaflet contends that "such definitions take precedence over any definition that may be found in the present commercial dictionaries, which have suffered periodical modification to please the powers in office."

"Shortly after the bank holiday in the thirties," the leaflet adds, "hush-hush orders from the White House suddenly demanded that all copies of this book be withdrawn from the Government Printing Office and the Army posts, to be suppressed and destroyed without explanation. This was the beginning of the complete red control of the Government from within, not from without."

Welch explains that a republic is the best of all forms of government because its rule is subject to "laws" rather than "men," while pure or representative democracy is government by majority vote and provides no protection for the rights of minorities against the "whims" of the electorate. The United States used to be a "glorious" republic—weak only in that it was subject to "fairly easy conversion" by demagogues and Communists into a democracy, "the worst of all forms of government." The conspirators are now at work piloting this malleable "mobocracy" into the treacherous waters of socialism and communism.

The gospel of Welch's talks is that the only salvation for the patriots of the nation lies in waking up to the danger and taking corrective action. This means alerting others to the Communist conspiracy and demanding action from congressmen and government officials. More important, it means doing it through active membership in the John Birch Society, whose leader's intuitive guidance provides the last and only sure chance for stopping the Communists before it is too late.

"You have probably never heard of John Birch. This is simply because the Communists in Washington planned it that way." This explanation is from the Society's Blue Book, the Founder's call to action against the entire "Communist conspiracy" in the United States.

Despite an impassioned biography of John Birch, in which Welch seeks to raise him to patriotic sainthood, Birch remains a little-known war casualty.

Captain John Morrison Birch was killed at twenty-seven by the Chinese Communists while on a mission in northern China, ten days after World War II had ended. The tall, handsome Georgian had gone to China as a missionary, became a chaplain with General Claire L. Chennault's Flying Tigers, and was inducted into the Army as a second lieutenant with Chennault's volunteers. He was both a religious zealot and a dedicated intelligence officer who knew the Chinese language and worked untiringly at the job of winning the war. He was given many hazardous liaison tasks and established close contacts with bands of Chinese guerrilla units.

Birch's last assignment was to Tsingtao. On the way, his

small group was stopped by a Chinese Communist patrol and the young American was killed. Some accounts, but not that by Robert Welch, indicate that Birch may have provoked the shooting. The Reds released the rest of his party later.

Some who knew Birch question whether he would willingly have lent his name to many of the precepts for which Welch's organization stands. But his death at the hands of Communists was sufficient for Welch to seize upon his life as a symbol of the kind of militant anticommunism its founder wanted the Birch Society to represent. In the portrait Welch painted, here was a sober, hard-working, courageous, moral, God-fearing American—an "angry saint" who had defied the Communists to the death. According to Welch, Birch was a martyr to the Cause and the first victim of World War III, which Welch says began with the end of World War II. Since Welch never met John Birch, his imagination was free to shape symbol to Society and vice versa.

Welch does much of his writing at the Society's headquarters in a neat, modern red-brick building on a quiet street in the Boston suburb of Belmont. The directory in the unimposing two-story office building lists the name *American Opinion,* which is the magazine of the Birch Society. The offices are those of both Society and magazine.

Forty-four persons were working regularly in the light, airy rooms of this humming headquarters in 1963, compared with the four-man staff that worked there for *American Opinion* before the Society was organized. Typewriters clack, duplicating machines whir, and telephones ring and ring. Secretaries scurry back and forth between the office and the Belmont Post Office next door with mail that requires $4000 a week in postage. The products of all this industrious effort are the monthly *American Opinion,* monthly bulletins to members (written by Welch), and stacks of reprints piled high on long tables in the main office. Reporters visiting the Birch headquarters are likely to be received with coolness. They are allowed to examine the printed offerings in the downstairs general office, buy, and leave. The head of the monolithic organization, ensconced in a private office upstairs, is too busy—by established policy—for interviews.

Welch's monthly bulletin is his pipeline to the Society's membership. This body of patriots, said the Chief Patriot in 1962, is composed of "tens of thousands" of persons—which could mean any number from 20,000 to 100,000. The latter is the highest estimate any Bircher has suggested. It was given by former Representative John H. Rousselot, California Republican, but actually the loyal, hard-core membership probably had not grown much beyond the smaller figure by 1963. Early in 1960, Welch has said, the total was 4000. More than two years later that remained the only figure he had revealed, though he claimed late in 1962 that "applications for membership are pouring into our office," presumably in reaction to Right-wing losses at the polls in the 1962 general election. Birch rolls are secret.

The bulletins list "projects for the month" that members must work on to demonstrate their fealty to the Cause and to get actively into the swing of Birchist anticommunism. All members are recipients of the bulletins—dues cover subscriptions. Bulletins in hand, members report monthly to living-room meetings in their neighborhoods. Except for invited "prospects," only members may attend. Depending on the financial status of the local leaders, monthly meetings are held in the comfort of suburban living rooms or in less imposing middle-class apartments. Cells are kept small, presumably for efficiency, by Welch *diktat*. They split before they reach memberships of two dozen.

A typical setting is the compact, moderately furnished living room of a dedicated chapter leader in a nondescript block of old duplexes on Chicago's North Side. Meetings begin at

8 P.M. the second Thursday of each month in this upstairs, back-entrance apartment. Early arrivals may peruse the collection of current and choice Birch literature displayed in the back-porch "library." All items are for sale or loan.

Assembled there one night in 1962 were the urbane and articulate host, in shirtsleeves; his quiet wife; half a dozen intense gentlemen in their twenties and thirties, including students; two plump, middle-aged women, one a secretary distressed by her boss' adamant refusal to see the noose the Communists were drawing around his neck; and two prospects. The meeting began, as usual, with a pledge of allegiance to the flag leaning in a corner. Then a card listing the plan of action for the previous month was passed around. Each member reported on what he had done to carry out instructions from headquarters. The chapter leader took notes and an assistant filled in a record chart on each person for his performance in each category.

The next order of business was instructions for the coming month. Everyone turned to the current bulletin, just arrived from Belmont. The discussion leader ticked off the orders—1 through 10—from Mr. Welch. (Members never omitted the *Mr.* in referring to the Founder.) Most important task: recruiting. Feel out potential members. A new recruiting tool was enclosed in the bulletin, a card with questions to be put to prospects. Its ten questions included combination statement-questions:

"It is clear that if enough good Americans came into The John Birch Society soon enough, our concerted effort could stop the Communists. Do you know of any other way, or chance, of stopping them?" In other cases the message was packed into the rhetorical question itself: "Are you willing to face facts now or, preserving your vested and protective interest in past error, remain among the willfully blind, who simply will not see?"

The other side of the question card had a list of *Have You*

Had Enoughs, such as "Enough of Senator Fulbright's program to muzzle our patriotic officers and demoralize our whole armed services?"

The next order of the day was to push *American Opinion,* which Welch reported had climbed in circulation to 15,000 but deserved much more because of its ability "to lay it out straight with regard to both foreign and domestic issues" and to "stand up against the inevitable vilification from the uninformed Right as well as the vicious Left. . . ."

Other projects for the month included reading up on how President Charles de Gaulle was selling France out and how the State Department was planning to disarm the armed forces in favor of a United Nations peace force "such as the one used in Katanga."

A flood of letters, "the only such flood we are asking for in this bulletin," was to be directed to "Senators, Congressmen, the White House, Secretary of State, newspaper editors, airwave commentators, and all the proper recipients . . . demanding that we get out of the United Nations for good." (The following month, red-white-and-blue bumper stickers were distributed, reading *Get us out of the UN and get the UN out of the U.S.*)

Efforts were to be continued "to build up a wide enough knowledge and understanding of what the Warren Court has been doing, so as to bring about impeachment of the Chief Justice." To this end, the members leaned back and listened to a long reading on record by L. Brent Bozell, an editor of the *National Review,* on the shortcomings of the "Warren Court."

Next the chapter leader collected dues and sold Birch and other Far Right literature. Before the members left to Read, Write, and Recruit, the record of a chapter from a Southern town was commended to their attention. That unit's accomplishments in 1961, in its own words:

Conducted a very active and successful campaign for the school board.

Started three new and very active front groups.

Arranged for over thirty anti-Communist speakers.

Written and paid for, over seven full-page newspaper ads on various issues.

Shown "Operation Abolition" to over sixty civic groups.

Shown "Communism on the Map" to over fifty-one civic groups.

Shown "Two Berlins" to twenty-one civic groups.

Shown "My Latvia" to nineteen civic groups.

Have loaned out 400 tapes to various groups for meetings.

Have elected seven members to program chairman jobs in various civic organizations.

Furnished nine speakers for out of town engagements.

Promoted an Indignation Convention and sent delegates to Dallas.

Have made and sold over 5,000 Impeach Warren bumper stickers.

Reproduced over 45,000 copies of various articles and mailing pieces.

Have promoted and found sponsors for the full year and coming year of these programs: Dan Smoot on T.V., Dan Smoot on radio, Fulton Lewis Jr. on radio, Independent American on radio, Manion Forum on radio, Layman Hour (local program) on radio, Party Line (local program) on two radio stations.

Paid expenses of our people to state PTA meeting.

Have four active study groups meeting weekly.

The report ended on the note that "our people are very conscientious about Bulletin requests" and "the influence our people have had on the scheme of things in our locale is staggering."

Welch gets monthly reports from all chapters. In addition, forms called "Member's Monthly Messages" detail what each member is doing and thinking. On them, members place orders for literature. They are encouraged to enclose contributions beyond dues. Members may include observations and suggestions concerning the "Americanist fight." The MMM system is designed in part to keep them on their toes and aware that their efforts are coming to the attention of Belmont.

The Society's position at the apex of extreme conservatism was won entirely by the efforts of its founder and leader. He not only proved himself an effective organizer, by employing self-styled "dictatorial" methods, but also showed an unequaled penchant for attracting notoriety. In writing in the privately circulated "Politician," or Black Book, that former President Eisenhower was "a dedicated, conscious agent of the Communist conspiracy," Welch was following his own Blue Book maxim that the way to alert the nation to the forthcoming Communist takeover was to "start shocking the American people." And when in reaction to this "shock," responsible people concluded that Welch belonged to the lunatic fringe, he protested that the remark was never the official position of the Birch Society. It had been intended for private use, he said, and the press, under Communist influence, was "smearing" him by printing it. He waded on with more of what he called "bombshells" and "absolute blockbusters," and made the Blue Book generally available. The major message of this bible of the organization is the grim assertion: "Unless we can reverse forces which now seem inexorable in their movement" there will be "only a few more years" before the United States "will become four separate provinces in a world-wide Communist dominion ruled by police-state methods from the Kremlin."

The "inexorable" forces are about to overwhelm the country because "Communist sympathies and even actual Communist subversion are daily made more respectable by the actions of our government, our great universities, much of our press, and by the complacency of our people."

In an effort to shake this complacency, Welch notes in his speeches around the country that the Communists "have molded every major policy decision in the American government since 1941 by their infiltration into high positions of power." He refuses to name names because he doesn't want to suffer the fate of the late Senator McCarthy, who was "smeared and destroyed" because he did so.

Welch assures his followers that "the truth I bring you is simple, incontrovertible." In both speeches and bulletins he follows McCarthy in singling out the clergy as among the worst of the treasonous influences on every hand. Three per cent (7000) of the nation's Protestant ministers, one half of 1 per cent of all Roman Catholic priests in the United States, and an unspecified number of rabbis are Communists or "Comsymps" (Communist sympathizers), he says.

When Monsignor Francis J. Lally, editor of the Boston *Pilot* (oldest Catholic diocesan newspaper in the U.S.), said the Welchian figure on Catholic Communists would add up to 273 priests and offered to print names and evidence, Mr. Welch had none. "This figure," he wrote Monsignor Lally, "is simply pulled out of a hat as a complete guess." But his accusation had already been exploited by followers who found it useful.

The John Birch Society, said Welch in the Blue Book, will use Communist techniques to fight fire with fire. Communist strategy, he explains, is to take over the nation "by a process so gradual and insidious that Soviet rule is slipped over so far on the American people, before they ever realize it is happening, that they can no longer resist."

One Communist tactic to beware of, he says, is a pretense

of favoring something so the United States will oppose it, or vice versa. Thus Premier Khrushchev pretended the Soviet Union was disgusted with the United Nations so the American people could "be made to overlook and forget the way the Communists are completely taking it over right now." "Let the Soviets demand that the United Nations be taken out of the United States," he adds, "and the American people will quickly forget their own rising wish to have this horrible Tower of Babel removed from our midst."

This is Welch's "principle of reversal." It can be used to explain anything that cannot be explained unreversed. For example, the real reason the Russians orbited the first Sputnik was to force the United States to increase its "wasteful" defense spending: "Although our danger remains almost entirely internal, from Communist influences right in our midst and treason right in our government, the American people are being persuaded that our danger is from the outside, is from Russian military superiority."

Defense programs are expensive and part of a Communist plot to sap U.S. strength. Welch explains that Russia would not engage in a shooting war anyway because it had been unable to conquer even little Finland. But hold on to personal firearms, he says. Calling for opposition to registration of guns, Welch notes that "as the Communists get ever nearer to taking us over . . . the pressure for this firearms legislation grows stronger." This is a Communist plan "to deprive us of weapons to whatever extent they can."

If any of this seems contradictory or difficult to unscramble, the self-styled Americanist provides an answer in the Blue Book: "Fantastic? Of course it's fantastic. But everything I am talking is fantastic." We are living in times, he says, when "it is realistic to be fantastic."

Part of the global plot is to ease into control of the United Nations and other international organizations. Western Europe "is either dying in front of our eyes or is already dead," so we can't expect much help from that quarter. Its strength has been "sapped beyond recovery by the cancer of collectivism."

The United States, where the international Communist conspiracy now finds "the backbone of its strength," is itself approaching collapse. Each year since 1958 Welch has rated the nations of the world on a scoreboard according to the "present degree of Communist influence and control over the economic and political affairs" of each country. Since 1958 the United States has climbed from "20 to 40 per cent" Communist control to "50 to 70+ per cent," and at that rate would reach saturation quickly. Israel is faring no better, and England and most other countries are even further gone.

Welch looks upon "the Roosevelt–Truman–Eisenhower–Kennedy Administration" as "one continuous administration under different names and fronts" that "have been striving so to change the economic and political structure of the United States that it can be comfortably merged in a one-world socialist government." Not since Herbert Hoover, then, has there been a non-Comsymp administration in this country.

Kennedy's 1960 opponent, former Vice-President Nixon, also left the Society little to cheer about. "He is one of the ablest, shrewdest, most disingenuous, and slipperiest politicians that ever showed up on the American scene," says the Founder. "As for being a leader, the sad truth, hard for many hopeful and wishful conservative Republicans to realize, is that Richard Nixon, a most engaging personality and clever politician, has never been a leader in connection with any event or development, or at any stage in his career."

Even so, the California Republican would be preferable to Governor Nelson Rockefeller of New York. "I think Nixon could become a very patriotic anti-Communist if we could create circumstances in which it would be smart politics to be one," the John Birch spokesman says. "I think Nelson

Rockefeller is definitely committed to trying to make the
United States a part of a one-world socialist government,
while I don't think Nixon is committed to anything other
than the career of Richard Nixon."

Welch has been harshest with Eisenhower. The antipathy
is deep-seated. Eisenhower forces, he wrote, "snatched" the
Republican nomination for the presidency from Robert A.
Taft in 1952. The undoing of Welch's favorite was accomplished "by purchase, theft, secret deals and other tactics
more foul than had ever before appeared in American politics."

The one man high on the political horizon who appeals to
Birchers at all is Senator Barry Goldwater. "He is absolutely
sound in his Americanism," Welch wrote. "I'd love to see him
President of the United States, and maybe some day we
shall." But if it were possible to elect Goldwater, he reasoned,
opportunism inherent in the political system probably would
make it impossible for him to stay the course with his Americanist supporters.

Is all hope lost, then? Must the nation fall prey to a Communist police state? No, says the transplanted North Caro-
linian to his readers and listeners; there is a way out: "The
John Birch Society now offers the one last best hope of saving our country and our civilization."

But it won't be easy. And it will take "dynamic personal
leadership around which the split and frustrated and confused forces on our side can be rallied, rapidly and firmly."
Where would the Americanists find the necessary "hardboiled, dictatorial and dynamic boss?" With McCarthy dead,
Welch felt that there was only one answer. Himself.

Hearing no objection from the eleven other charter members at the meeting in Indianapolis in 1958 at which the Society was founded, the new leader laid down ground rules
for a campaign to stop communism in its tracks and make
it possible to go on from there to the group's long-range

objective of "less government, more responsibility and a better world."

How to combat a cunning enemy? Exposure. Where to look? Everywhere. Parent-teacher associations, college faculties, the pulpit, government, the press, unions, libraries. "One of the hardest things for the ordinary decent American to realize is that a secret Communist looks and acts just like anybody else," the Blue Book says.

How to spot a non-Americanist, then? "Now there are ways of sizing up both individuals and organizations in this battle," the Founder counsels, "which come only with experience . . . and a feel for the way a Communist works." He says he knows from the way his opinions check with those of J. B. Matthews, former executive director of the McCarthy investigations subcommittee, "that I have a fairly sensitive and accurate nose in this area." "And of course I also have the benefit of J. B.'s files, almost incredible memory, and judgment built out of long experience," he adds.

Matthews lost his post, over Senator McCarthy's objections, after charging that "the largest single group supporting the Communist apparatus in the United States today is composed of Protestant clergymen." That unsubstantiated assertion, President Eisenhower held, portrayed "contempt for the principles of freedom and decency."

For future exposure, the Society has asked its members to build up the most complete files in the country on "the leading Comsymps, Socialists and liberals." Welch said in a 1962 bulletin that "these are the files we are going to need before we can ever give the whole truth—or enough of it to save our country—to the American people."

Although the American Communist Party claimed only 10,000 adherents at the time and has lost membership since, the bulletin estimated that there were 300,000 to 500,000 Communists in the United States, plus "not more than a million allies, dupes and sympathizers."

It might reasonably be presumed that Welch, using his nose for such things, would decide which of these to expose. But anyone who counted on such help in tracking down the enemy would very likely be as disappointed as the Department of Justice was. In 1961 Welch made a speech in Austin, Texas, in which he said ". . . a comparatively few thousand Communists, concentrated in key departments and agencies of our government, could do—and I believe have done—a terrific job of determining both the policies and the actions of those agencies and departments—and hence indirectly of our whole government." Whereupon the Department of Justice wrote Welch demanding that he supply the FBI "at once such facts as may be in your possession and the sources thereof which you believe establish that certain government employees are members of the Communist Party." Welch was forced to concede that he knew of no Communists in the government. Finding them, he said, is the job of the Attorney General.

When pressed to explain their failure ever to uncover a Communist despite the abundant supply, Birchers sometimes cite Red cleverness at concealing true colors, a menace of the menace. While the Society might never be able to prove a person was a Communist, Welch says in the Blue Book, sometimes it can get "all the material needed for quite a shock." With such material, he says, "we would run in the magazine [*American Opinion*] an article consisting entirely of questions to this man, which would be devastating in their implications."

Welch concedes that "the question technique, when skillfully used in this way, is mean and dirty," but adds that "the Communists we are after are meaner and dirtier and too slippery for you to put your fingers on them in the ordinary way —no matter how much they look and act like prosperous members of the local Rotary Club."

"Mean and dirty" might likewise be applied to tactics So-

ciety members have used to disrupt public meetings. At a
gathering in a public school in California, for example, a film
and public discussion were planned. Seventy to eighty John
Birch Society members attended and broke into cheers or
boos on signal. Whenever a speaker mentioned democracy
they shouted *republic!* The state's attorney general, Stanley
Mosk, said they interrupted and insulted the audience and
speakers. At a meeting of a club in Encino, California, he
reported, seventy-two Birchers became so abusive in their
interruptions that it was necessary to call the police.

Yet George Barrett, a *New York Times* reporter who followed Welch on a trip through the South, found the John
Birch leader acutely sensitive to the possibility of being heck-
led himself. During one address, an attendant started to look
for a physician. Nervously Welch stopped his talk to ask why
the man was "walking around like that." Without pausing for
a reply, he told the audience the distraction was a typical
"dirty Communist trick."

Welch has no scruples in pressing his campaign against
anyone he suspects of Communist inclinations. In Wichita,
Society members have reported on "Communist influences"
in the classroom and then directed concentrated telephone
attacks at educators considered less than superpatriotic. The
library there became another target.

The Birchers' campaign against the nation's clergy has had
the desired effect in many localities. As fundamentalists,
some elements of the Society oppose preaching of a "social
gospel" that attempts to relate biblical teachings to secular
problems. Society members are thus particularly critical of
the National Council of Churches, a group that often favors
liberal social legislation. In Amarillo, Texas, the Birch leadership said it would continue to stir up friction in local
churches until ministers conceded that the National Council
had been infiltrated by Communists and agreed to do something about it. And in Santa Barbara, California, members of

the First Presbyterian Church received a mailed Birch Society "questionnaire" attacking its leadership and that of the National Council.

These Birch activities have stirred spirited reaction. Senator Stephen Young, Ohio Democrat, has been one of many to denounce the Society as a "fascist group." He told the Senate: "Unfortunately, these radicals of the Right in the so-called Birch Society in many communities have been practicing character assassination without regard for the truth, threatening merchants with boycotts, threatening college professors and school principals with dismissal. They spread fear, hatred and suspicion."

Birchers pressured a chain store in Glenview, Illinois, a village-board member there reported, to stop selling Polish hams. Welch ordered in the December 1961 bulletin that members protest the sale of such hams ("slave labor merchandise") by the Jewel Tea Co. of Melrose Park, Illinois, "or by anybody else." Earlier, a drug chain had been urged to stop selling whisk brooms made in Hungary. Welch called their sale an example of "treasonous infiltration" of Communist merchandise "into our economy."

The campaign mushroomed in 1962. A Miami group formed the Committee to Warn of the Arrival of Communist Merchandise on the Local Business Scene. It held "card parties," surreptitiously slipping small cards into displays of merchandise at grocery and department stores found to be selling anything made in Communist countries. "Always buy your Communist products at [name of store]" was a typical legend, printed in red. A Welch bulletin praised the committee and urged Birch Society members to "help make the drive national."

"For those conservatives who really want action this is like the answer to a prayer," he said. "It is effective and it is fun!"

Soon card parties were held from coast to coast. Some

merchants resisted the pressure; others acquiesced quickly. In Dayton, Ohio, a major retail and mail-order chain store stopped selling ham, wine, glassware, bicycles and jewelry made in Communist-ruled countries. In Fort Wayne, Indiana, a supermarket publicly burned 700 offending wicker baskets. In further retribution, it took a large newspaper ad pledging never again to "display nor offer for sale to our customers any merchandise known to be a product of a Communist Nation," but rather to uphold "the American System of Free Enterprise" and "the American Way of Life." In several cities ordinances were passed requiring stores selling Communist-made imports to pay special fees and post signs saying "Licensed to sell Communist products."

Part of the program of action ordered by Welch is "organizing Americanist fronts for many different purposes." "The front business, like a lot of techniques the Communists use, can be made to cut both ways," he says. He orders Birchers to "organize fronts—little fronts, big fronts, all kinds of fronts."

The Birch fronts have specific purposes. Whether they reveal their Birch affiliation depends upon the cause. The Society is proud to have its name associated with such a front as the Movement to Impeach Earl Warren. Welch even conducted an essay contest with prizes for college students who turned in the best-reasoned manuscripts on why the Chief Justice of the United States should be removed from his post. "The Supreme Court as a whole in the last few years has been engaged in destroying the Constitution of the United States," he said in announcing the contest. He believes the Court has been usurping the legislative function reserved to the Congress. Elaborating in a bulletin, Welch wrote: "Earl Warren, while probably not the most powerful man on the Supreme Court, has been its Chief Justice during the whole period of these decisions which have given the Communists so much aid and comfort. . . ." First prize of $1000 in the essay contest was awarded to a young Californian who favored the impeachment not only of Chief Justice Warren but of Associate Justices William O. Douglas, Hugo Black, and William J. Brennan as well.

With the campaign to impeach Warren, Welch says, "we have carefully chosen a very vulnerable spot of the enemy, against which to launch this determined and sustained attack. For there is simply no way that the Comsymps and Liberals can defend the actions of the Supreme Court since Warren became Chief Justice without making clear to any informed observer that what they really want is to change completely our whole form of government and destroy our marvelous inheritance."

Condemning Warren makes good sense to the Radical Rightists because Warren headed a Court that not only ordered racial integration of the public schools but also handed down a series of decisions counteracting McCarthyism: the federal Smith Act supersedes state antisedition legislation; congressional investigating committees are limited to fulfilling legislative purposes; federal loyalty restrictions must be limited to employees in sensitive posts; persons being tried for federal crimes may inspect the confidential government files being used against them; and so on. In addition, the liberal faction of the Court, including the Chief Justice, has supported a long line of reforms in civil liberties and in government, such as the 1962 decision favoring reapportionment of seats in state legislatures to correct inequalities in voter representation. Welch believes that these are subversively democratic decisions which show Chief Justice Warren up for what he is.

No cause is too small if it can ferret out a "Comrat," Comsymp, or even a dupe. For example, Welch suggested that a Committee to Investigate Communist Influences at Vassar College would make a likely front group. And when the airlines serving Indianapolis happened to be struck at the time of Welch's 1958 visit there, the inconvenience prompted him to suggest a Petition to the Airplane Pilots Association to Grow Up. "It is obvious that some Left-wing influences," he said, had crept into the association in considerable strength.

Other Welch-decreed tactics for alerting the nation to the Communist peril, or smoking out Reds wherever they might be hiding or infiltrating, include wide dissemination of "Americanist books" and pamphlets. Welch urges volunteers to set up and man rooms similar to the Christian Science reading rooms. These *American Opinion libraries*" may vary "all the way from a mere sun porch in somebody's home to an actual store on a busy street," he suggests. Efforts must be made, he says, to increase the circulation of conservative periodicals such as *American Opinion, National Review* (before it tried to read Welch out of the Movement), the *Dan Smoot Report,* and *Human Events.* The new libraries, most of which are bookstores, sell the periodicals as well as "books on our side"; some have become nerve centers for local Birch activity.

In matters of discipline and tactics, Welch's pattern is totalitarian and geared for action. "It is imperative that all the strength we can muster be subject to smoothly functioning direction from the top," he wrote in the Blue Book. "No collection of debating societies is ever going to stop the Communist conspiracy from taking us over, and I have no intention of adding another frustrated group to their number. We mean business every step of the way." He made it clear from the beginning that he would have no truck with the two-sides-to-every-question idea or "so-called democratic processes," and added that "those members who cease to feel the necessary degree of loyalty can either resign or will be put out."

With annual dues of $24 for men and $12 for women (life memberships $1000), revenue from the magazine, and contributions, the John Birch Society was able to count on $1,600,000 a year to work with as early as 1961.

Welch considers effective organization the key to success, and has appointed "major coordinators," "coordinators," and "chapter leaders." By 1962 there were thirty-five coordinators on full salary and expenses. There were seventy serving without pay or for partial remuneration. Coordinators are responsible directly to headquarters, and Welch's grip on the reins of his network of local chapters is as tight as he can make it. Members are obliged to accept their assignments without question through the Welch chain of command. They get no accounting of dues or contributions.

The coordinators' work has been particularly fruitful in Texas, which has had as many as 150 chapters. California ranks with the Lone Star State. Other pockets of strength are scattered throughout the country. Shreveport, Louisiana, Jackson, Mississippi, Los Angeles, and Houston quickly became Birch centers. Cells formed and multiplied in many of the larger Midwestern cities and their suburbs.

Birch organizers are not content merely with the direct approach. Sometimes without identifying themselves as Birchers, they encourage civic clubs, church groups, and PTAs to sponsor addresses or a series of lectures on communism. At the suggestion of the still-unidentified Birchers, participants at the lectures may form study groups. When such a group decides to explore all angles of the Communist menace, the Birchers suggest that the Society be invited to make its presentation with the hope that some conservatively oriented members of the study groups may be attracted to the Welch banner. That, at least, has been a pattern in some of the more prosperous suburbs of major cities.

As does the Birch Society's general membership, the organization's National Council includes prominent businessmen. Their names are printed and circulated to lend prestige to the Society. The Council, as Welch put it, also has the function of selecting "a Successor to myself as head of the John Birch Society if and when an accident, suicide or anything sufficiently fatal is arranged for me by the Communists"—or if the Founder simply dies.

Three former presidents of the National Association of Manufacturers have served on the Council—William J. Grede, the late Cola G. Parker, and Ernest G. Swigert. So has T. Coleman Andrews, Commissioner of Internal Revenue during part of the Eisenhower administration and States' Rights candidate for President in 1956.

Andrews' pet project is abolition of the income tax, and Welch is with him on that. In a recent bulletin, he counseled his followers that "we believe it is now time for us to start putting our support more energetically behind the campaign" for a proposed constitutional amendment that would repeal the Sixteenth Amendment and hence abolish the personal income tax. As Welch put it, the proposed amendment "would force the Federal government to sell its hundreds of businesses now competing, at such huge annual losses, with private industry." In the Birch view, the income tax would no longer be needed "because of these tremendous savings in Federal expenses." Welch believes that "without the revenue and regimentation of the Marxian graduated income tax, the Liberals could never have established their present increasing tyranny in Washington, and even now could not maintain it."

Another evil is foreign aid. Spruille Braden, former ambassador to Colombia, Cuba, and Argentina and an original Birch Council member, has called the United States foreign-aid program counter to religion because it benefits atheistic Communists and their henchmen. Welch agrees. The "very idea of American foreign aid was dreamed up by Stalin, or by his agents for him," he has written. Braden, who long represented big business in South America before turning diplomat, considers Welch a "very personable" friend as well

as a "devoted, dedicated patriot." Braden joined the Birch
Society because "it was the one organization I saw that
seemed to be alerting people to the danger of communism
at home and abroad in an effective way." As vigorous an opponent of Fascists as of Communists, Braden does not agree
with some of Welch's views: that a U.S. President was a
traitor, that Trujillo fostered liberty, and the like. He believes
that the Founder should proceed with more care in speeches
and in print or confine himself to organizing.

Fred C. Koch, a Wichita oil-company president who
serves on the Council, is interested in "right to work" legislation to prohibit the union shop. Welch blesses the right-to-
work movement as "patriotic."

The Founder's authoritarian leadership has attracted
persons to whom a "Little Hitler" has appeal. His sermons attract the sincerely concerned as well as the gullible.
The wide-ranging scope of his ultraconservative interests
also attracts some community leaders able to exert influence
at the local, state, and national level. Most of them share his
opposition to the majority of programs, foreign or domestic,
that require expenditure of federal tax money. Birchers lump
most social-welfare programs together as costly steps toward
a welfare state that will make the country ripe for painless
merger with Soviet communism.

It is often a matter of rugged individualists trying to hold
on to as much of their wealth as possible. Other Birch members sincerely fear that cherished liberties will end if government gets any bigger. Among the latter are some members of
the medical profession. An editorial in the *Wisconsin Medical
Journal* expressed the editor's dismay "that prominent medical men in several communities have associated themselves
with the John Birch Society causes."

Welch's audiences are of two types—both conservative.
One is composed of dedicated and prospective Birchers.
They get the pep talks, the build-up-the-membership-to-

save-the-country message. Welch addresses them at private meetings, frequently informal gatherings at homes of members. Here he lets his guard down somewhat, adopts a confidential and even jovial air, but never fully casts aside suspicion. Even such a meeting as this might be infiltrated. His appearances at private sessions have decreased a great deal since the early organizing days.

Welch also speaks at public meetings—to Far Right groups, civic bodies and conservative political groups. He accepts invitations when possible despite the heavy work load at headquarters, in order to make converts and to replenish the Birch coffers with sizable fees.

The core of respectable citizens on Birch rolls in some communities gives the Society sufficient status to win it a hearing despite the scoffers. For determination and organization the Society ranks at the top of the superpatriotic heap. It has taken advantage of a resurgence of less wild-eyed conservatism to push its own viewpoint, but refuses to compromise with other Rightist groups to form a united front. Welch refuses to unite, that is, unless a unified organization accepts a single dynamic leader named Welch.

"Now we are surfeited in this country today with organizations opposing Communism or socialism," the Founder of the John Birch Society wrote in the Blue Book. What is more, he added, even if all of the hundreds of Right-wing groups were combined into one organization "for the very purpose of obtaining centralized coordination," the unified effort would be "grossly inefficient" unless "the members of these groups declared allegiance to, came to feel an unshakable loyalty for, and thus accepted direction from, a dynamic personal leader."

As the "hardboiled, dictatorial and dynamic boss" said of his Society—and, since he is the Society, of himself: "Nowhere even on the horizon does there appear any other force with sufficient character, understanding, determination and cohesiveness to have any chance of stopping the Communists." He has stoutly maintained his messianic view despite the counsel of such conservative leaders as Senator Goldwater that he resign for the good of the organization because of his discredited exaggerations. He has clung to his creation despite a crescendo of denunciation from the more responsible Right.

One of the most devastating broadsides came early in 1962 from an influential conservative spokesman Welch had counted on for continued tacit support. In an incisive editorial in the *National Review*, William F. Buckley, Jr., said Welch was "damaging the cause of anti-Communism" by distorting reality. The editor, a thorn in the side of the Liberal Establishment ever since he wrote *God and Man at Yale* a year after graduation from college, called on conservatives to reject the Bircher's "false counsels."

Buckley pointed out that it was a crucial misapprehension to assume that Welch's excesses concerning Eisenhower and others in the Black Book were merely personal speculations with no bearing on the Society and its activities. He noted that Welch had never disavowed the book, that his writings in fact continued to support its central thesis that "the government of the United States is under operational control of the Communist Party," and that this was the view that continued to govern his thinking and guide his practical leadership of the Society.

Buckley wrote that "by the extravagance of his remarks" Welch was splitting the conservative movement, giving it a black eye, and inhibiting the growth of his own Society: "The John Birch Society...is growing no faster than the movement to impeach Earl Warren, who remains as unimpeached today as when Mr. Welch first launched that ill-conceived campaign. Mr. Welch, for all his good intentions, threatens to divert militant conservative action to irrelevance and ineffectuality."

This shaft at the "fog of confusion that issues from Mr. Welch's smoking typewriter" was only one of many from the Right. Senator John Tower of Texas, a pillar of the Right, labeled the Buckley editorial an "airtight case" against Welch and inserted it in the *Congressional Record*, associating himself with its conclusions. And Senator Goldwater, after advising Welch to "burn" the Black Book, suggested that the Society reorganize under different leadership. Also voicing dissent was Russell Kirk, prolific defender in print of the conservative viewpoint. He wrote that Welch, "by silliness and injustice of utterance," had become "the kiss of death" for any conservative effort. Kirk wrote of "a general effort of enlightened American conservatives to reform or else cast off the political fantastics who have been clinging to their coattails."

Welch was shaken by the public denunciations from non-extremists on his own side of the fence. He was tense in disclosing the then still-forthcoming Buckley editorial to a small group of his supporters after his Milwaukee dinner speech. He repeatedly lifted both hands, fingers taut, to his head in a tearing-the-hair gesture. Some people on the Right have failed to grasp the full scope of the problem, he said. In his next bulletin he explained that the Communists, as any self-respecting Welch disciple surely knew anyway, again were responsible. Just as they had coined the phrases "I like Taft, but he can't win" and "I like what McCarthy is trying to do, but I can't stand his methods," he said, they were now bruiting the idea that the John Birch Society could do a lot of good if it got rid of Welch. In other words, the Communists were using recognized spokesmen of the Right to discredit Welch, their "major enemy."

"It is only because the Communists are able to devise such reasonable-sounding slogans and then to get good anti-Communists to spread these slogans for them" that they are effective, Welch wrote. Bruised but unbowed, he rejected the suggestion that he step aside. If he did, he said, the Society's strength would disappear.

But he was badly hurt, and showed it in pique. "If our Right-wing critics think that we are going to be crushed by their jealousies and their sniping," he wrote, "they are as wrong as the Communists. . . ." He added in a tirade against "eggheadism" on the "uninformed Right" that rivals of the Right were "stirring up friction and resentment. . . . These egotists do not even begin to understand the loyalty and dedication and determination of our members."

He assured his followers that Buckley's editorial would soon be forgotten. As for Kirk, he "soon gets lost" when he "leaves his Ivory Tower and wanders into the rough terrain marked CONSPIRATORIA." Welch excused Goldwater's denunciation as political and said "most of us" would "gladly" vote for him anyway, but counseled that "the good Senator is off base when he starts trying to run The John Birch Society from the outside."

The whole imbroglio is a dastardly scheme of the "Libs" to throw all anti-Communist forces into "snarling confusion," he said. "An important aim of the whole present campaign is to bog me down with infinite explanations *to our own people,* while the mind almost breaks down at the magnitude of the job that needs to be done." The anguished emphasis is Welch's.

But with a studied turn of the other cheek, the anti-Lib dipped into a thesaurus of quotations and brought forth Edwin Markham's noble strategy as a formula for combating his tormentors:

> He drew a circle that shut me out—
> Heretic, rebel, a thing to flout.
> But Love and I had the wit to win:
> We drew a circle that took him in!

Goldwater, Kirk, and Buckley form an articulate triumvirate of the Respectable Right whose basic beliefs match those of the Far Right in many cases, but who refuse to attribute sinister or subversive motives to more liberal contemporaries who disagree with them. The Respectable Right is willing and able to participate in the national dialogue on the democratic basis of free speech and debate without resorting to hysterics and name-calling. Because Welch has not done this, the trio publicly unfrocked him of respectability within his own wing, and he has been on the defensive ever since. The Birch argument used for years to explain away the Welch vilification of Eisenhower—an argument contending that criticism of Welch for a 1958 view was outdated—had been exploded by reason. Despite the caliber of its membership in many cells, the Society's claim to respectability, so long as it took its orders from Welch, had been brought under serious question by the organization's friends. Many Society members solved the problem for themselves by praising Welch for those views with which they agreed, as well as his organizational skill, while reserving the right to disagree with him about Eisenhower.

Welch conceded that the intramural controversy was "disturbing our membership at large" in a way no accusations from "liberals" could. He conceded that even some members of the Society's National Council tended to agree with his detractors. But Welch was not to be easily derailed. The niche he had carved on the Radical Right was his niche. The monolithic society he had created was his society, prosper or collapse. There was no successor in sight. Members who didn't like it could adapt or get out. Whether his "respectable" supporters had paused to figure it out or not, Welch was obviously on the extreme fringe of the Far Right and intended to stay there.

In this endeavor, his most devoted followers would support him to the end. This was evident in the "Dear Bob" letter of February 15, 1962, written under the letterhead *Edwin A. Walker, 4011 Turtle Creek Blvd., Dallas 19, Texas.* "There are many rumors that you will be or are being placed under great pressure to step out or up," it said. "Either would be equally detrimental. Do not do it under any circumstances. Any member trying to change your title status or position in any way is wrong. You are the Birch Society."

The former major general who lost his command because of his fervent espousal of Birch principles signed the note "Sincerely, Ted." The recipient gave it a full page in the bulletin and accepted the advice.

4:

'Enry 'Iggins
of the Right

The bright-eyed, bouncy man on the platform seemed to
vibrate with energy. The cadence of his speech was almost
hypnotic. His punchy, shrill oratory first had listeners rising
from their seats, then he relaxed them, had them turning to
their neighbors, smiling, nodding their heads, even giggling.

It was almost 11 P.M., and the speaker in the auditorium
in St. Petersburg, Florida, was finishing:

"I want to get down to the real business. How much money
are you going to give us? I'll tell you what we're going to do.
At your seat you've got an envelope and we want you to use
this for your offering. Now if anyone hasn't got one we didn't
mean to insult you. We're sorry. Please forgive us. We'll get
you one straightaway. On this check form put down the
name of your bank and the branch. Put down the amount of
money and sign your name. You say, 'How much do you
want us to give?' Well, that's simple. How much have you
got?"

The audience broke into easy, relaxed laughter. The speaker smiled and paused. He looked around, but he wasn't through. "We don't want one dime more. Not one dime more than you've got. We don't want the check bouncing. . . . 'Ask and ye shall receive.' So I ask. Have I made myself clear? Have I asked? Have I left anyone in doubt? Now just give what you can, and if you haven't got a pen, borrow one."

The speaker was Dr. Frederick Charles Schwarz, forty-nine at the time, a short, lively, dark-complexioned man with just a trace of puffiness about his face. His brown eyes sparkle and dart as he cajoles and shames and humors his audience into giving.

And they give. The 1961 take for his Christian Anti-Communism Crusade was $1,273,492, more than three times the total for 1960 and greater than the combined receipts for 1953 through 1960. The crusade slipped a bit in 1962, largely because a major effort for the year, an attempt to stir up support in New York City, fell flat.

Fred Schwarz is twice a doctor; once in medicine (University of Queensland) and once in theology (honorary, Bob Jones University, Greenville, South Carolina, Bob Jones, Jr., President). An Australian who has applied for United States citizenship, Fred Schwarz is also a psychiatrist of sorts as well as a lay preacher in the Australian Baptist Church. But he is much more. Schwarz has become the hottest campaigner on the professional anti-Communist circuit, employing showmanship and accent that have, in the words of one observer, made him the 'enry 'iggins of America's Right Wing.

Since he came to the United States to stay, in 1953, Schwarz has been selling anticommunism from a headquarters at Long Beach, California. Talks in small southern California churches started him; a session as an "expert" before the House Un-American Activities Committee moved him into the big time, and he is now supported by multimillion-dollar corporations and sponsored by local committees set up wherever he goes with the aid of Schwarz advance men. Schwarz comes into a city with his "faculty" and opens an anticommunism "school." Lectures and literature-for-sale are the marks of the meetings, built around sessions that run day and evening for two, three, four, or five days, with a banquet or a public rally thrown in for good measure and good income. Between sessions of the school Schwarz may appear at civic, professional, or industrial meetings as a solo speaker, often without fee.

Schwarz is sensitive to charges that he is a patriot for profit, but he is always selling something—a book, a recording, a pamphlet. At the end of an evening in St. Petersburg, as at sessions in other cities, Schwarz wound up the meeting talking fast and selling hard:

"Now people say, 'I want to study communism, where do I start?' Here, of course, is where I come into fundamental conflict between honesty and humility." With barely a pause, the speaker resolved the conflict. He straightened, smiled, then leaned forward again over the lectern: "I always say, 'Begin with my books.'

"Here's a book that you can trust, *The Communists* [*You Can Trust The Communists (To Do Exactly As They Say)*]. It's had a tremendous reception. Many of the lectures I give in the morning you'll find in this. Now it costs you two ninety-five in the shops. We give you a special price—three dollars." As if on cue, the audience snickered with delight.

His enemies, he went on to say, are either unaware of the evils of communism or are at best unwilling dupes of the conspiracy. But Schwarz never misses with his "I have nothing to hide" appeal:

"You see, when people talk about you, they've got to manifest their own natures. People say you are avaricious. Why? What they mean is if they were doing it they'd be greedy for money, therefore we must be.... There's no way of convincing your enemies, so don't worry about our enemies. It's

our friends that worry me more. I'll tell you this right now.
With regard to the money situation, my salary is $5,000 a
year. That's what my salary is. Now all the royalties of my
books go to the Christian Anti-Communism Crusade. There
are about $20,000 each year. All my speaking fees go into the
Crusade, and just recently there were $2,500 for just one
week."

His voice was rising, his Down-Under accent becoming
more pronounced.

"All our books are audited. We publish the audit and in
Los Angeles we made a profit of $200,000. How dreadful!
How wonderful! We're proud of it. . . . Now I try to be me-
ticulously honest . . . my salary is $5,000 a year. My wife is
secretary of the Australian Crusade. She gets four-fifty a
month. The rest of it goes into the work of the Crusade. Now
I'm no martyr. I've got enough. It's not my ambition to be
the richest man in the Communist liquidation line."

Peals of laughter rolled through the auditorium and Fred
Schwarz was grinning. He had them, and he took advantage
of it: "What we want you to do is this. Work with us. Cooperate with us. Get on the phone, double the crowds here."

Schwarz has a thirty-man staff that prepares rallies and
operates the Long Beach headquarters and a branch office
in Houston. In 1961, administrative costs—including salaries
—were listed at $223,788.

Schwarz became president in 1960, succeeding W. E.
Pietsch upon his death. Schwarz and Pietsch, an old-time
Waterloo, Iowa, radio evangelist, had incorporated the Crusade in Iowa in 1953. Schwarz says that on his first visit to
the United States he met Pietsch, who invited him to "come
back and start a Christian anticommunism crusade." Schwarz
always ran the Crusade from Long Beach, even though the
older man was nominally president and had, in 1956, moved
to Long Beach to be closer to the headquarters.

That year the Crusade was granted tax-exempt status as

an organization "operated exclusively for religious and educational services."

The Schwarz literature table, set up wherever the Australian speaks, makes money at dime-store prices. Besides paperbacks and pamphlets for a quarter and up, there are "Midget Missiles," which he calls "excellent envelope stuffers," for a nickel, and "Penny Projectiles" ("Brainwashing With Ink," "Hangman's Noose," etc.) for one cent each. There are also comic books explaining Communist ideology ("We believe this answers a great need"), and a "How to Establish a Local Study Group" manual.

Besides the paraphernalia and prattle of political evangelism, what does Fred Schwarz offer?

In April 1961 he brought his show, with its ten-man faculty, into St. Louis for four days. He had already put on programs in Philadelphia, Dallas, Los Angeles, and elsewhere. The St. Louis rally was typical of the many yet to follow. School was in session at a hotel some distance from downtown. Schwarz called the production the "Greater St. Louis School of Anti-Communism."

Attendance at lectures ranged from 200 to 600 people, and reporters covering the week-long session were struck by the number of boys and girls of high school and college age in attendance, as well as by the preponderance of couples under forty, small businessmen, ministers, salesmen, teachers, and middle-class housewives.

Schwarz and company had been invited by the customary committee organized under the guiding hand of a Crusade advance man. The names of sixty sponsors appeared on the program, including those of the mayor, two United States senators, the chief of police, and some prominent manufacturers, bankers, and merchants. Two local organizers of John Birch Society chapters also were listed, and Governor John Dalton proclaimed an "Anti-Communist Week in Missouri."

Schwarz has been able to enlist respectable sponsorship

more often than other Right-wing operators, although frequently—after the schools have adjourned—the sponsors have been surprised to discover what they have lent their names to.

Fred Schwarz is his own star attraction as well as ringmaster and between-acts salesman, but he has a full cast of supporting players. A few are regulars on the payroll of the Crusade. Others are migrants of the Far Right. They travel from one lecture platform to another between dates with organized road shows.

Herbert (*I Led Three Lives*) Philbrick, former undercover man in the American Communist Party for the FBI, is one. Two of his topics are "Communism and Youth" and "Cybernetic Warfare." Robert Morris, former chief counsel for the Senate Internal Security Subcommittee and former president of the University of Dallas, sometimes participates. So does W. Cleon Skousen, former Salt Lake City police chief. Besides Schwarz, ten to a dozen speakers, often including a congressman or two, are listed as the faculty for an anticommunism school. The faculty may be different for each "school." Former Congressmen Rousselot and Edgar Hiestand of California and the Birch Society have been faculty members. So have Representative Gordon Scherer, Ohio Republican, and Senator Thomas Dodd, Connecticut Democrat. "The only answer to total defeat in the struggle against Communism," warns Dodd (a former FBI man), "is total victory."

The titles of the talks offered by the various faculty members vary, but the basic line is the same: the planned attack on and destruction of the "moral fiber of America" by agents of international communism. Schwarz says that 1973 is the target date for the Communist takeover in America, although he fudged on that at a 1962 rally in New York's Madison Square Garden, making it "within twenty years." And although he himself never states it explicitly, some members of his "faculty" usually make it clear that the takeover will come because of "the enemy within."

The danger, the audiences are told, is from subversion in many segments of American life. Speakers cast suspicion on the Kennedy administration, the Supreme Court, liberals, racial integrationists, the United Nations, large sectors of the Protestant clergy, the World Council of Churches, professors, and "intellectuals."

Although Schwarz speaks most, he says least. He talks of Christian morality and details the struggles for power within the Communist Party. He is anti-Communist, pro-American, and in favor of good as opposed to evil. He carefully avoids name-calling.

What does Fred Schwarz think of his own activities? "I'm always amused when I read these articles that talk about Right-wing revival," he says. "They talk about the Radical Right. They talk about extremists. Now I don't know what they are talking about half the time because nobody has bothered to define what they mean by the term 'Right,' as far as I'm concerned. I don't know whether they mean it in the political sense. I assume that if they meant that we have fascism that we would want to set up a political party that was small and compact and disciplined with military overtones. Well, if that's what they mean, it is utterly and completely and entirely false ... I say that we are Christians and that we are anti-Communists and that is where we stop."

What about responsibility for the statements made by other members of his Crusade "faculty"? Does he agree with speakers who stand against everything from a national mental health program to the fluoridation of water and for the repeal of the income tax and the impeachment of Chief Justice Warren?

"I feel the responsibility for the selection of the faculty. I accept that responsibility and I accept the basic responsibility for the basic content of the school. However, within this framework, I do grant to the faculty members academic freedom. I don't make every one of them provide a script which I edit and say, 'You can't say this, you can't say that.'

When the school begins I announce that every individual is free to make his own proposals for discussion. Some of them won't be acceptable so far as I am concerned."

Schwarz says the only job he wants to do is teach. Does he consider Philbrick, Skousen, and other regulars qualified educators?

"I consider they have a contribution to make and that the basic tone and spirit is in tune with the school and its message," he replies. "It doesn't mean that I agree with every specific proposal that they may make."

One instructor wants a top-to-bottom investigation of the State Department; another wants American membership in the United Nations reconsidered. Does Schwarz agree?

"I do not necessarily approve of them personally . . . the individual has a right to advocate these things. He has the right to suggest them . . . insofar as my own personal position —I deliver more messages than anyone else—I believe I set the general tone of the school and when I'm asked questions concerning specific national programs my usual reply is, 'I can't answer that because what we do in this area depends on what we're going to do in that area . . . and until we have a very complete picture, it's very difficult to answer specific national problems in isolation.'"

Is Schwarz pleading discretion, lack of conviction, or ignorance? Again he has his own answer, phrased with the apparent candor that has given him so much success.

"Well, I'd say it was ignorance. I don't know everything. . . . I don't think I lack conviction . . . especially when it comes to the nature of communism, its plans, its purposes. I simply don't know the answer to every question of national and international policy that the situation demands."

On certain broad issues Schwarz does not hesitate to express himself. "People say to me: 'Should we negotiate an agreement with the Communists?' I say: 'Should we swim backstroke to the moon?' They say: 'Your question is stupid.'

I say: 'So is yours.' Because if communism is communism, and I believe it is, an agreement is simply an instrument of warfare for our conquest."

When reporters in St. Louis called his Anti-Communism Crusade a "poor man's John Birch Society," Schwarz fumed. The comparison with radicals of the Right enraged him sufficiently to make him fire angry letters off to publishers. The comparison, he says, is part of a "smear" that he believes is a Communist plot to discredit militant anticommunism.

Schwarz does not make clear his feelings about Robert Welch and the John Birch Society. Although many of his associates are also involved in Birch affairs, Schwarz says, "I don't know very much about the John Birch Society."

Told that Welch has said the Birch Society seeks to "recruit people who have been stirred up, awakened and alarmed" by him, Schwarz replied, "That is his privilege."

He adds: "I know a lot of John Birch Society members. Very fine people, indeed, most of them. Very democratic, very dedicated, very concerned about communism . . . I can't judge motivations. I don't believe in trial by newspapers and condemnation by reporters. I've suffered a little bit that way myself. Maybe the John Birch Society has suffered. . . . Along with, I hope, other intelligent people, I will reserve a measure of judgment."

Few are reserving judgment on Fred Schwarz. Those who approve think of him as wise and well-informed, helping to lead a moral revival in the United States by prompting an awakening "before it is too late." Crusade officers estimate that as a result of Schwarz' efforts more than 5000 "study groups" have been formed. Others consider him a pitchman, a hypocrite, a professional in the art of preying on public fear and suspicion for financial reward.

The Christian Century says: "The country has plenty of colleges, universities, magazines, newspapers and study groups which inform people accurately as to what the goals

of communism are and what we must do to defeat these
goals. But they do not call these efforts 'crusades' and they
do not raise immense sums each year by playing on people's
fears. Dr. Schwarz uses the methods of political revivalism
to generate a state of mind in which people are unable to
teach or learn anything."

Schwarz' Australian twang, amiable personality and hard
sell did not take hold all at once. The Fred Schwarz who
holds an audience in St. Louis, Oakland, Columbus, New
Orleans, Omaha, New York, or the Los Angeles Coliseum
has traveled the twisting road up in what is a reasonable
facsimile of the American "success story."

Frederick Charles Schwarz, son of an Austrian immigrant
and an Australian mother, was something of an "energetical"
Christian while still a youngster. He and his brothers and
sisters grew up in Brisbane and went to school there. He
enrolled at the University of Queensland and, he says, in
1940 met his first real Communist, a man he identifies as
Max Julius, a lawyer and member of the Central Committee
of the Australian Communist Party.

Up to that time, says Schwarz, he had not started to
argue with Communists from any political basis but more
on a philosophical plane—"the dignity of man and the
purpose of life" were his interests. So when he engaged in
a debate with Julius in 1940, "Max made a bit of a monkey
out of me on that occasion and stimulated my interest and
I read more profoundly of the Communist doctrine and the
works of Marx and Engels, Lenin and Stalin." He kept on
debating with Communists until, Schwarz says, the Australian Communist Party laid down a policy that none of its
members might meet him in debate.

Schwarz was studying other things as well. He finished
college, then medical school, and established a modest practice. He continued to study psychiatry and at the same time
worked as a Baptist evangelist—a lay preacher. He also

taught mathematics at a teachers' college, and found time to marry and start a family. His wife and children live in Australia.

Schwarz might still be there, as a full-time doctor and part-time preacher, had not a series of events brought him to the United States. He tells how it happened:

"I was active in the Evangelical Christian circles and belonged to the conservative theological school and two Americans visited Australia ... Carl McIntire, who's president of the American Council of Christian Churches, and Dr. T. T. Shields from Canada, and I helped arrange their meetings, which was normal enough for me in those circumstances."

(McIntire, dropped from the Presbyterian ministry for violating his vows of ordination, has his own evangelical anti-Communist radio program and fundamentalist following.)

Schwarz says the visiting churchmen became interested in his ideas on how to fight communism and soon he was invited to the United States to speak. It was 1950 and Joseph McCarthy was being heard in the land. At first Schwarz confined his efforts to a few small churches and eventually returned to Australia. But he had made "contacts" and came back to the United States in 1953, when McCarthyism had become a preoccupation for many Americans.

In Southern California, where the extremism of the Right was well nourished, Schwarz gained powerful financial and public support.

In 1957, he appeared before the staff of the House Committee on Un-American Activities. Under the respectful questioning of Richard Arens, staff director, he described the nature of communism. None of the congressmen on the committe was present. It didn't matter. The appearance gave him stature; the record of his testimony amounted to the closest thing to a testimonial that the committee could give.

Schwarz' testimony was reprinted and copies were distributed by the tens of thousands by the Allen-Bradley Company of Milwaukee. Since then, Schwarz says, the manufacturer of automatic controls has continued to contribute about $10,000 a year to the Crusade.

In 1962 Schwarz added to his credentials in anticommunism when the United States Information Agency arranged for distribution of *You Can Trust the Communists* abroad.

He had also attracted national attention in 1960, when the banner of his Crusade was unfurled over the Hollywood Bowl. Twelve thousand people were in the audience and perhaps four million more saw and heard the show over thirty-three television stations in six states.

The production was all Hollywood. John Wayne, George Murphy, James Stewart, Pat O'Brien, and other stars of the screen were on hand. Besides Schwarz, the speakers were Senator Dodd, former Representative Walter Judd of Minnesota, and the publisher of *Life* magazine, C. D. Jackson.

Earlier that year, in an assessment of Right-wing groups, *Life* had categorized Schwarz and his troupe with Birchers and other extremists. In an editorial the magazine said "Schwarz preaches doomsday by communism by 1973 unless every American starts distrusting his neighbor as a possible Communist or 'Comsymp.'" The crowd applauded wildly when Jackson publicly made amends to Schwarz for "an oversimplified misinterpretation" of the motives of the Christian Anti-Communism Crusade.

Later *Life* said, in a modifying editorial, "Dr. Fred Schwarz is himself well informed and his Christian Anti-Communism Crusade attracts much respectable support, but it also attracts people who are too superheated to teach or learn anything."

Schwarz says that his first big contributor was Patrick J. Frawley, Jr., who heads Technicolor Corp., and the Schick Safety Razor division of Eversharp, Inc. Schwarz opened an envelope one morning and found a check for $5000 from

Frawley. Thereafter, Frawley has been one of the Crusade's most consistent backers.

The cost of televising the Hollywood affair, nearly $50,000, was borne by the Richfield Oil Company, Schick, and Technicolor. A spokesman for the advertising men who handled the three-way sponsorship said the "response has been gratifying."

Technicolor and Schick also bought three hours on WPIX, a New York television station, to replay the program for the benefit of New Yorkers. Before it was shown, ads appeared urging, "Wake Up To The Dangers of Communism." The speakers were listed and so were the "Endorsers of This School: George Murphy, Pat Boone, Ronald Reagan, James Stewart, Nat 'King' Cole, Connie Haynes, John Wayne, Robert Stack, Jack L. Warner."

Schick has since backed off a bit. A New York distributor of Schick products, learning of the company's support of Schwarz, said he would not help support "such a vicious gospel through the profits of my sales." He started taking Schick products out of the 400 supermarkets he served in the New York City area. They went back on the shelves after Schick's president, Thomas J. Welsh, wrote the distributor that it was no longer his company's policy to buy television time for Schwarz' Crusade because it had already made its "patriotic effort."

Welsh added, though, that "we still think very highly of Dr. Schwarz' Crusade."

New York saw a good deal more of Schwarz in 1962, but hardly took him to its bosom. The Crusade lost $75,000 on a rally in Manhattan Center, another in Madison Square Garden, and a five-day "Greater New York School of Anti-Communism" that filled only a small fraction of Carnegie Hall's 2760 seats.

Aside from publicizing Fred Schwarz, what has the Crusade done?

When it left St. Louis, responsible citizens were concerned. They felt the meeting had troubled the city and might encourage extremists of the Right to launch new campaigns of harassment.

A charge in several cities has been that Birchers move in to organize, insofar as possible, the "students" who attend Schwarz schools.

In Florida some of the sessions were piped into classrooms on an educational television system. The propriety of this was heatedly argued. Those who opposed it said the instructors did not measure up to the state's educational standards and should not have been allowed to use state educational facilities for political propaganda.

During the 1962 anticommunism "school" in Oakland, one of Schwarz' sharpest critics was Attorney General Mosk. He called the seminar a fly-by-night promotion and, when asked for an apology, repeated the charge.

"These promoters," said Mosk, "have not produced evidence that their so-called school is qualified as such under the laws of any city or county, or that any of the alleged instructors have teaching credentials issued by the state of California. Thus this is a promotion and not a school. That it is fly-by-night is demonstrated by its nomadic character. The operation moves from city to city where the financial pickings are best."

Schwarz is, essentially, a peddler of phrases. He has perfected the use of ambiguity. "Are those who fight racial discrimination Communists?" he was asked on one occasion. "No," he told the all-white audience, "please don't think that everyone fighting racial discrimination is a Communist." His audiences read their own meanings into his torrent of words, enjoy his showmanship, and pay him to keep up the good work.

5:

Billy James Hargis and the Christian Crusade

What is beneficial to one "anticommunism crusade" will not long be ignored by another. Simultaneously with the Oakland spectacle put on by Fred Schwarz, the Reverend Billy James Hargis conducted his own Christian Crusade's "first annual national anti-Communist leadership school" in Tulsa.

While this affair included large public rallies at which admission tickets were sold, "classes" were limited to 200 "students" at a "tuition" of $100 each for the week. For this and the names of industrialists who might support Christian Crusade, the students were promised insight on what they and their communities could do "to stem the forces of liberalism and thus stop the growth of socialism and communism."

Clearly the star performer of the faculty was Billy James himself, a rotund hellfire evangelist who turned much of his tract-and-rostrum talent from religion to anticommunism

69

when, his detractors contend, he learned that implanting fear of Reds meant more dimes and dollars than preaching fear of God.

"Put it up to a vote of the people," he thundered at the seminar in a typically pointless generality, waving an arm with an abandon that puts Robert Welch's puny gestures to shame, "and the people would overwhelmingly vote against the Communist Party U.S.A.!"

The assertion was neither profound nor debatable. But the way he said it—the emotion-packed voice, the slamming of the enemy, the haranguer's emphasis, and the final shout— all guaranteed the ringing applause and cries of "Amen!"

The 270-pound, moon-faced young evangelist manipulated his audience for half an hour. As he warmed to his work, calling foreign aid and participation in the United Nations a sin, his face reddened, his head bobbed, and his jowls shook. "I must demand," he shouted in a voice that carried beyond the mezzanine of Tulsa's Mayo Hotel, "that the Attorney General of the United States prosecute the individual Communists of this country . . . or resign!"

The noisy response was nothing new for the young founder-director of the Christian Crusade. "I know how to handle an audience," he had said privately earlier.

No one could disagree. Good use of this talent, from the broadcast studio as well as the soapbox, has made the Christian Crusade, like Schwarz' Christian Anti-Communism Crusade, a million-dollar business.

Hargis has become immunized to attacks on his tactics and to charges of money-grubbing. He has a blanket rejoinder. "Our friends know, whenever they read any attack against Christian Crusade or me, that it was born in Moscow and is a part of Khrushchev's plan to smear and discredit any patriot that lifts a finger against the dangerous trend in America towards socialism and Communism."

The evangelist, son of a truck driver, was born in Texarkana, Texas, in 1925. His formal education ended with a year at Ozark Bible College, then in Bentonville, Arkansas. He was ordained as a Disciples of Christ minister while still a teen-ager and held pastorates briefly at Sallisaw, Oklahoma, Granby, Montana, and Sapulpa, Oklahoma.

Billy James founded his Crusade in 1948 and, to devote full time to it, left the Sapulpa church two years later. At first he concentrated on exposing what he felt was a trend in Protestantism away from fundamentalism and toward a "modern" or "social" gospel. But it was not until after Hargis hired L. J. "Pete" White, Jr., as his public relations adviser in 1955 that business improved sharply.

White, owner of the White Advertising Company in Tulsa, was an old hand at preacher promotion, having helped to put Oral Roberts, a Pentecostal Holiness minister, in the multimillion-dollar bracket.

Despite national notoriety, Hargis is neither knight nor oracle in his home town. Roberts still casts a much larger shadow in Tulsa, much to the chagrin of Billy James. There is not a cabbie in Oklahoma's second city who could not drive directly to Roberts' Abundant Life building, but there are few who could find the downtown Christian Crusade headquarters without guidance. Tulsans know about Billy James but have not adopted him. When he sought to build a proper headquarters to compete with Roberts for a place in the Tulsa sun, residents of his chosen area protested and the city planning commission zoned him out. "A prophet without honor here," his public relations man complains.

The first year White handled the Crusade account, its billings were $40,000. Six years later they were ten times as much. White's concern gets a 15 per cent commission plus a flat fee.

Hargis gets $12,000 a year, plus his considerable expenses. He also gets two cars and a $43,000 "parsonage"—a beautiful Tulsa home where he lives with his attractive wife Betty

Jane and their six children, all of whose names bear the parents' B. J. initials. They have a 700-acre ranch seventy miles north of Tulsa.

The Hargis operation now carries the same message of peril from internal Communist treachery as does that of Welch. The evangelist reaches millions through radio, television, tracts, pamphlets, newspaper columns, newsletters, magazines, and books. It is perhaps the most prodigious non-stop promotional venture ever heaped on the shoulders of one man.

Billy James writes a weekly column on the threat of communism that is published, he says, in more than 200 newspapers. He produces the *Weekly Crusader,* a newsletter on the dangers from Communists within this country that has a circulation of some 10,000 copies and a subscription price of $10 a year. An ad for it pledges "startling developments" and "revelations." He publishes and writes a good part of *Christian Crusade, the National Christian Americanism Monthly.* It reaches 100,000 Hargis followers who subscribe at $1 a year. The annual output is also available in a bound volume, with the purchaser's name printed on the cover in gold, for $5. He writes innumerable pamphlets on any subject in the news, from General Walker to Katanga, that he can relate to communism. Each sells for $1, although there are bargain rates for bulk purchases of 25 to 500 copies of any one title.

"Announcing brand new patriotic pamphlets by Billy James Hargis," screams one advertisement in the monthly magazine. "New material, new design, new approach to getting inexpensive but truthful anti-communist information to the masses. Ideal for mass circulation to churches, schools, civic clubs, fraternal groups, etc. We are constantly endeavoring to make available to Crusaders factual anti-communist publications for mass distribution. We judge by your letters what subjects you are most interested in."

The judgment produced, for this ad, such titles as "The United Nations—Destroying America by Degrees," "The Communist Program for the American Farmer," "Walter Lippmann—Poisoning Public Opinion," and "Uncle Sam— M.D.?" The latter was described as a "timely article on federal aid to the aged, which is merely a foot in the door for the complete socialization of medicine."

Billy James is never coy about plugging his own booklets. On the back of one he lists and describes others:

> "Communism and You." An excellent first lesson in the methods and aims of Communism. 25¢ each, 5 for $1.
>
> "We Have Been Betrayed." The stirring address delivered by Dr. Hargis at the National Congress of the D.A.R., April 1961. 35¢ each, 3 for $1.

He explains that "as you know, there is a real effort on the part of many publishers, book reviewers, columnists and book sellers to prevent the publication and/or distribution of any pro-American books," and he urges, "Help overcome this blackout by the enemies of America, give widespread distribution to this important literature."

Hargis frequently tells his reading and listening audiences that "regardless of what anyone says, our greatest problem today is internal communism." To add a note of urgency, he informs one and all that the Kremlin has set 1974 as the deadline for conquest of the United States. "Clean up communism internally," he wrote in a brochure called "What's Wrong With America?," "and America's problem with communism internationally will be solved."

On forays into international issues, he is prone to overreach while sensationalizing a point. "When in a few months Gizenga becomes head of the entire Congo Government and openly declares himself a Communist as did Castro just a few days ago," he wrote in December 1961, "our

liberal intellectuals in Washington will raise their eye-
brows in surprise and wonder just what happened. Readers
of the *Weekly Crusader* will not be surprised." By the time
Hargis had set for Gizenga to take over, the Congolese leftist
had been deposed as vice-premier and was being held in
protective custody. But Hargis was not in much danger of
being checked on; he can count on many of his insulated
followers to do little reading about international affairs.

He sometimes plays on ignorance. "Even today, according
to the U.S. Information Agency," he wrote in "We Have
Been Betrayed," "less than 4 per cent of the total population of 215,000,000 Russians are members of the Communist
party . . . if Communism and/or Socialism is so wonderful
as many liberals seem to think, why haven't the people who
have lived under this system since 1917 accepted it by now?"
He has become adept at using the old McCarthy technique
of the half-truth, in this case implying that party membership is available to all Russians.

Some of his wild statements about the United Nations
have even less basis in fact. "Many well-informed persons
have reason to believe that the United Nations Charter was
written by Alger Hiss and Molotov," he wrote in the *Weekly
Crusader*. "In essence, it is taken almost entirely from the
phony constitution of the Soviet Union." As for Berlin, "it
is a headache to Nikita Khrushchev and his ambition to
occupy the White House before he dies."

"I love to write," Billy James said one day. "I believe in
the power of the pamphlet." One of the most powerful
pamphlets he has produced was used in 1960 in an Air
Force manual as documentation for a charge that Communists had infiltrated the Protestant clergy. The National
Council of Churches responded that Hargis was an op-
portunist capitalizing on fear of communism for his own
aggrandizement. The manual was withdrawn with apologies

to the National Council by the Secretary of the Air Force
and the Secretary of Defense.

Billy James says there are more than 1000 of his booklets
and pamphlets in print. "We know we'll sell at least fifty
thousand copies of anything I write," he told a visitor.

In 1960 he branched out again, producing the first of a
series of books, *Communist America—Must It Be?* This was
hailed in a Crusade brochure ("Facts About Christian Crusade") as "recognized by many experts as the most valuable
primer on anti-Communist efforts ever published." Another
Crusade ad calls it "one of the most illuminating books on
the Communist menace yet published, clearly written and
easy to understand."

The ground covered in *Communist America—Must It Be?*
is considerable, despite the lack of detail, as can be seen
from a glance at some of the chapter headings: "A Free
Press—Leading America Leftward," "Patriotism—Once Re-
vered, Now Smeared," "Communist Influence in American
Schools," "Communism and Labor Unions," "The Suicidal
Folly of American Business," "Communism and Racial Tension," "A Supreme Court Against America," "United Nations
—the Greatest Hoax Ever Perpetrated on the American
Public," "Fantastic Foreign Aid," and "Communism and the
National Council of Churches."

To help in his research, Billy James has at his Tulsa
headquarters what he describes as the most complete library
of Communist publications extant. He concedes, however,
that he hasn't had much time to browse in it. This did not
impede the broad strokes of his conclusions in *Communist
America—Must It Be?*

"The Communists win every battle they engage in," he
wrote. "Every decision of the United Nations, every action
of the United States, and most free nations, seem to help
advance the cause of aggressive godless Communism."

The enemy is upon us and the consequences of our insane failure to awake to the danger of almost certain defeat is horrendous to contemplate: "So clever has been the Communist intrigue, and so successful has its subversion within America been, that the capture of the world's freest and richest nation lacks only another shove or two. Spying, infiltration and treason continue at an alarming rate. . . . There will be paralysis of our communications, transportation, money and law enforcement systems. Finally there will come direct seizure of power by the agents of the Kremlin within America. . . . If the average American citizen doubts that his beloved country is in mortal danger, that his wife and children are on the verge of the embrace of Communist rape and enslavement, let him look anywhere about him."

Hargis notes that "when the uninformed are first made aware of the Communists' advancements inside the U.S.A., one of the first questions they invariably ask is 'Why haven't I heard this before?' "

"The answer is simple," he explains. "For the most part, America's daily newspapers [he specifically excluded Westbrook Pegler, then a Hearst columnist and later a columnist for *American Opinion,* the Birch organ] are promoting the Communist Line."

Treason does not end there, however. Congress also is "leaning heavily to the left-wing, pro-Communist side." In fact, Congress is only one step from final surrender to the intruders. "Abolishment of the Un-American Activities Committee is a major goal of the Communists," Billy James writes, "and if they succeed in achieving this goal, we will then be at the complete mercy of the Communistic conspiracy." Some departments of the administration have already succumbed. The Communists have turned the Department of Health, Education and Welfare, for example, "into a Kremlin-directed base for the subversion of three vital American pillars—health, education and welfare."

"Not since 1935" have the Communists had to look outside the United States for the funds they need to effect all this infiltration. "Much of these funds are supplied by American business," Billy James reveals. "Biggest of all contributors is the United States government, at the insistence of American business."

Why American business has sold out is not clear from reading *Communist America—Must It Be?*, but the result is obvious: "America—and the American people—today are practically powerless against the enemy. The people of the United States have ceased to be their own rulers—and the government now ruling them is heavily pro-Communist."

Hargis also informs his readers of the true nature of the United Nations—"an important part of Communism's carefully conceived and brilliantly executed plan to destroy America and the free world." He finds the organization suspect from the beginning because its meetings are not opened with prayer. "Instead," he reports, "in the main corridor of the New York Headquarters, there is a statue of the mythological Greek god, Zeus, the destroyer of virtue and womanhood, who raped his own mother."

Also packed into this informative volume are the revelations that foreign aid "is destroying America"; that "Marxist teachers are being implanted in schools everywhere"; that the nation has drifted to socialism; and that "Socialism and Communism are one and the same."

Lest any reader despair, however, the epilogue hints at a ray of hope. If "Americans who are willing to sacrifice to keep their freedom" will contribute enough money to anticommunist bulwarks such as the Christian Crusade, there may yet be a way out. "It is only through this help that such organizations are able to continue to fight against Communism, for these organizations depend entirely upon the contributions received," Billy James warns. The back cover notes that even though "the powerful, liberal church-related National Council of Churches has sought to smear and discredit him . . . Dr. Hargis carries the crusade against Communism to the Nation unflinchingly and courageously."

The "Doctor" derives from honorary degrees conferred on the evangelist by Defender Seminary in Puerto Rico and fundamentalist Bob Jones University. His aides usually address him as "Doctor" and all the literature distributed by the Crusade accords him that title.

Hargis said he could not get his work published by any publishing house so he bought his own, formerly the Higley Press of Butler, Indiana. With it he acquired rights to "thousands" of religious books, which Christian Crusade now offers in package deals of various kinds beginning at "25 per cent off" until demand slackens, then, in subsequent ads, for half price. Package sales of these books are "a good deal," Hargis said candidly, "because we don't have to guarantee any particular titles."

The Crusade also distributes, at a profit, many other books. One ad in a recent issue of the organization's magazine proclaims that "Christian Crusade is proud to offer a fabulous publication of the John Birch Society, entitled 'A World Gone Crazy.'" The blurb says "All 107 countries of the world are viewed under a microscope, and the degree of Communist influence and penetration in each is exposed in this fearless book. When you read this charge of dynamite, you will understand why the forces of hell and liberalism are out to discredit the John Birch Society—a fine, patriotic group with the courage to print the startling truth in 'A World Gone Crazy'—not available to the public elsewhere. Only $1. We have only one thousand! First come, first served!"

It is the same shrill, carnival-barker prose used to entice the credulous to Hargis rallies. HEAR THE DARING, AUTHENTIC FACTS ABOUT RED INFLUENCE! shouted a headline in an ad for "Two Great Meetings Tomorrow!" in Los Angeles. A DIFFERENT SUBJECT EACH SERVICE: COME AND ENJOY A REAL

CHRISTIAN AWAKENING. The circus pitch also is used to sell all manner of Crusade-conceived commercial items. "Crusader seals," bearing the slogan *Fight communism, support Billy James Hargis and Christian Crusade* over a picture of a Crusader on a horse, go for 25 cents per sheet of 100. The persuader: "A Christian Crusade Seal on every piece of mail that leaves your home or office will have a great impact on the many hands it passes through en route to its destination. Attractively printed in red, white and blue. . . ."

Bumper stickers in the same colors, at four for a dollar, testify to the superpatriotism of the driver of the car.

At Christmastime the Crusade has seasonal suggestions. "Dr. Billy James Hargis has personally selected this year's official Christian Crusade Christmas cards," subscribers to the magazine are informed. There are choices, such as "Glad Tidings," "the finest card money can buy in the famous Sunshine Line. Only $1 a box . . . no limit to number of boxes you can purchase. (Postage free.)" There is "Scenorama," "the first Children's Card we have ever offered!" This also is available in unlimited numbers. "Coins that Jesus Used" is a de luxe card mounted with facsimilies of coins from the Middle East of 2000 years ago. $1. For those who would like something a little more elaborate, "Dr. Hargis' friends in Jerusalem have sent him a new shipment of Olive Wood New Testaments," the covers made of olive wood "taken from trees in the vicinity of the Garden of Gethsemane." $3.

"We can get people to buy anything we tell them to," White, the public relations man, said. While sale of merchandise brings in $200,000 a year, contributions, the Crusade's biggest source of income, provide more than three times as much. For this, Dr. Hargis' most potent appeal is through the spoken rather than the printed word. By radio, television, and personal appearances he reaches millions in the course of a year. He claims half a million "Crusaders"

—anyone who has ever contributed is counted, and is also permanently on file at Crusade headquarters on address plates for resolicitation purposes.

The evangelist's broadcasts always praise "God and Country." The initial appeal is religious. It finds its most fertile field in the fundamentalist Bible Belt that Hargis has known and exploited ever since he left Ozark Bible College. Many fundamentalists are not concerned solely with Bible fundamentalism, the heresy of liberalism, and atheistic communism; they are also concerned with the growing trend to racial desegregation and equality, the election of a Catholic President, and with social changes that are upsetting the tenets they have prized from childhood. And they are deeply concerned, especially the wealthy and middle-class fundamentalists, that they are being excessively and unfairly taxed to support unwanted do-gooder, pro-minority, and pro-labor government programs.

Many Hargis followers may be gullible, but many others are not. The latter realize that Doctor Hargis' methods are less important than whether he is effective in serving their ends. If he can frighten the fearful and appeal to the prejudices of the illiberal and uneducated and thereby throw roadblocks in the path of liberal progress, he is worth supporting with the pocketbook. Hargis followers, rich or poor, have no difficulty accepting the conspiracy theory of social change. There must be a simple explanation for the assault being made upon their long-established values. The Hargis explanation—Communist subversion in our midst—is confirmed by the pronouncements of such other heroes as Robert Welch and Edwin Walker. The religious, social, and economic fundamentalists in kitchens and offices throughout the Hargis country often are securely in the fold. They have been subjected, in Hargis broadcasts and pamphlets, to one of the greatest "educational" barrages in history.

For the benefit of the masses, the Hargis theme is kept

simple. Lack of education is no handicap to understanding that God is good and that Communists—likely to be anywhere—are evil. The crudities are unnoticed or overlooked by the faithful. Even at the 1962 Tulsa "anti-Communist leadership school," with a faculty of varied talents supplementing the Hargis line and filling the air with unsettling charges of treason, few "students" got more than the basic message. The reaction of an Oklahoma City housewife was typical. Did she find the seminar valuable? "I'm glad to see people are waking up." To what? "The Communists are here." Where? "Everyplace." Have you run into any? "I don't know any personally. But the value of the meeting was to educate people as to what goes on."

For any who are similarly vague about what to do when they return home, Billy James spells out the answer in a red, white, and blue pamphlet entitled "A Call to Action to Every Real American":

"Listen to the splendid broadcasts of Dr. Billy James Hargis, Fulton Lewis, Dean Clarence Manion, Dan Smoot, Dr. Carl McIntire, Martha Rountree, Dr. Wayne Poucher and Paul Harvey.... Distribute pro-American literature.... Make your patriotic views known to office holders, community leaders and others.... Join Christian Crusade at once!"

Under a subheading "Join This Great Effective Organization," Billy James says, "You will be proud to be a part of the country's leading organization of its kind. Christian Crusade is the largest, fastest growing and most active organization in America solely devoted to combating Communism."

If this is true, Billy James is not satisfied. He is fired with an ambition as great as his bulk. "At first I wanted to be pastor of the largest Christian Church in the United States," he said. But that was before he found communism. Now he works day and night to expand his influence as arch-foe of the common enemy. His vision is fully as messianic as that of rivals Welch or Schwarz. "I have built this mass movement," he says. Then, remembering that he first reaches 80 per cent of his supporters with a religious appeal, he corrects himself: "God has built this movement through me."

Along with mother, father, wife, children, and friends, *Communist America—Must It Be?* is dedicated to God, "who saved me and used me for a purpose." Billy James is pursuing the purpose at a pace that would put many men in an early grave. In addition to his voluminous writing, most of which he does by dictaphone at his desk, he broadcasts weekly over more than 200 radio and television stations throughout the country. The number has grown steadily since 1955, when he started. Most of the broadcasts are recorded in the Crusade's headquarters studio. Tapes are banked for future use, because the evangelist is on the road twenty days a month for speeches, rallies, and promotions. The tapes, of course, also can be purchased, attractively boxed, at $5 each.

By 1962 Billy James had nine radio broadcasts a week. Seven were fifteen-minute daily programs and two ran half an hour each. One was carried over the Mutual network. Others were placed with independent stations. They reached nearly every state. The Crusade has found it profitable to buy radio time because the largest percentage of its $650,000 a year in contributions can be traced to the broadcasts. No broadcast is without an appeal for financial aid to continue the battle against the swelling tide of communism in the United States.

The biggest advance came with the addition of fifty-five stations on Mutual in 1961. Billy James raised the money to buy twenty-five minutes on the network once a week for the first twenty-six weeks by conducting a prayer auction at a convention of the Crusade in Tulsa a few months before the broadcasts began. The cost was $38,870.

"I need four men who will accept God's challenge and give ten thousand dollars each to sponsor this program," he told the assembly.

Two men stood.

"Give us four, Oh God, who would give five thousand dollars each. Quickly! . . . two thousand dollars?"

One man stood.

"One thousand dollars?"

Three stood.

As the requested amounts decreased to $100, more contributors rose, until seventy-nine men and women had pledged the total needed.

The Crusade later expanded to television. In 1962 it offered fifteen-minute weekly filmed programs carried by at least a dozen stations. Billy James is the star performer, but he also has other Right-wingers as guests. And as explained in a Crusade brochure, "Color or black and white prints are available for church and educational use at special rates."

Tapes of anti-Communist addresses are "a big sell," Dr. Hargis said, as he was showing a visitor his wares.

Besides records of his broadcasts, he can now be heard, for $5, on a record reading chapters of *Communist America —Must It Be?*

Billy James also sings, and this talent is tapped in a record called "Songs and Sayings of Billy James Hargis." It offers "pure, beautiful gospel music plus a homey visit with Dr. Hargis" in a "folksy album" that "combines the spiritual and the patriotic." "Beloved hymns" are combined with "the stirring God Bless America and Battle Hymn of the Republic," packaged in an album cover done in "beautiful, four-color living color!" Stereo, $5; monophonic $4.

Wherever Billy goes, the books, records, and pamphlets go. Stalls are set up outside the speaking halls. There is something for everybody, from five-cent pamphlets to $15 books. Reprints from *American Opinion* are included. Pic-

tures of "the Doctor" also are on sale. One, in a gold frame
at $6.50, meets every need of the Hargis-oriented patriot.
It shows the evangelist behind his desk. In evidence in
his hands, on the desk, or nearby are the American flag,
a statue of a Crusader, the Constitution, and a picture of
Christ.

Billy James says he is on the road two-thirds of his life.
He holds rallies throughout the South and Southwest and
is eager to expand his influence to the North and East. He
travels in a bus, rented for $867 a month, that looks like
a modern Greyhound. For Billy James it is a home and office
on the road; here he eats, sleeps, and labors. In 1961, the
bus carried him 46,000 miles through thirty-six states.

The bus sleeps five, although sometimes "the Doctor" and
his driver make trips alone. Billy's quarters in the rear are
living room by day and bedroom by night. The wall-to-wall
carpeting is mustard color and some of the upholstery is
bright orange. The bus has every convenience that limited
space will allow—two telephones, recording facilities, two
baths and a shower, plenty of closets, and a well-stocked
stainless-steel galley.

The Crusade has an advance man on the road all the
time, arranging for rallies. By the time Billy James arrives
the book stand has been set up. "Free will" offerings are
taken. Billy James speaks for an hour.

"For the first ten minutes I give them old-fashioned faith,"
he said, describing the operation. "Then we have fifty
minutes of anti-Communism." He shakes more hands than
most politicians. "You've got to get out and shake hands. I
believe in personal contact."

He said he could not build a movement sitting in his office.
When he returns from a sweep across the country, he sees
that letters go out to everyone who signed in at any of his
meetings.

"My creed is follow-up," he explains.

At the Tulsa headquarters he has fifty employees. Four women read and classify the 2000 letters that come in daily from persons who have heard Billy James. All but about 100 can be answered by one of thirty form letters. Billy James tries to reply to the rest himself. He says his postage bill is about $150 a day.

Hargis pulled out a wire basket stacked high with letters, segregated because they had contained no contributions. "We're glad to get this free mail," he said a bit ruefully. "They're all new prospects."

All will get replies. Some will join the average of 10,000 new "crusaders" (contributors) the Christian Crusade claims to be getting each month.

Although the Crusade has wealthy backers, in oil and other industries, most are not rich and their letters contain only a few dollars. The name and address of each contributor finds its permanent niche in the office files. All contributions to the "ministry" are tabulated in the organization's "banking department." Every day an armored truck takes the proceeds to the bank.

Letter-answering, with renewed appeals for funds, is done with electronic equipment in eight-hour shifts by day and night crews. Most money appeals stress that small donations are welcome and needed. But Hargis cannot resist fishing for higher stakes from time to time. In one pamphlet he pointed out:

"Assignment by Crusaders of stocks, bonds and other properties have increased measurably and are welcomed as this ministry proceeds to its inevitable destiny of coming to grips with any and every pro-Communist or subversive influence in America." Such appeals usually note, as this one did, that "Christian Crusade has been recognized by the United States Department of Internal Revenue as a national, tax-exempt religious organization. All contributions to Christian Crusade are deductible from the income tax of the contributor."

Hargis' plush private office is filled with gifts of crusade statuary, made mostly in Europe. He has become a collector. Some of the pieces are junk, others are valuable. In fact, the headquarters is so full of mementos, such as a statue of Joan of Arc and an old sword carried through the Crusades, that the evangelist plans a full-fledged "Liberty Museum" to contain them. It also will contain tributes to patriots from Washington to McCarthy. The founder-director of Christian Crusade envisions it as a "showplace of Americanism."

As with everything else the Crusade does, the showplace will have promotional value. "We've had every kind of promotion available," the corpulent evangelist said. He even hailed the adverse publicity the Far Right has received. "It hasn't hurt us a bit," he said. "These attacks prove to the people that what we say is true. They think, 'These men must really be effective in the fight against Communism or they wouldn't be attacked.'"

Another feature of the Crusade headquarters is its "research and intelligence" department, which includes the library his staff uses in research work for his books. It includes "everything the Communists ever put out." Hargis also claims "we have a file on every Communist worker and every minister and professor and labor leader with Communist affinity ever branded subversive by a Government agency."

He said the library contained 5000 books on communism, pro and con. One of its treasures is the complete collection of Allen Zoll, long notorious as an anti-Semitic spokesman.

The breadth of the appeal of the Christian Crusade is illustrated by its 1962 "school" in Tulsa.

One lecturer, R. Carter Pittman of Georgia, sought to prove that Negroes were inferior to whites in mental capacity. He ascribed efforts to integrate schools to a Communist conspiracy. He said Negroes were not patriotic and invariably "stampeded" in battle. The chief difference between Congolese and Negro American soldiers, he said, is that the Congolese eat more white people than Americans do. Twice he used the word *niggers*. Most of the "students," including members of Southern white citizens councils, stood and applauded when he finished.

"He really did a grand job," said one man. "He sure had the facts," said another. "I could have sat here and listened all night," said a woman.

Hargis made a show of dissociating himself from the Pittman lecture. Before it was delivered he said no "extreme" or "bigoted" statements would be tolerated. But he also said he would not censor faculty speeches because that would be "totalitarian." When the Pittman class was about to begin he left the room.

He was not so cautious with Revilo (Oliver spelled backward) P. Oliver, a member of the National Council of the Birch Society. Oliver, a Texan, is a professor of classics at the University of Illinois. His attentions to race were more subtle than Pittman's. He used such terms as *mongrelization* and drew laughter by referring to the Freedom Riders as "young punks who have replaced the boll weevil in the South."

Oliver also brought to Tulsa the Welchian principle of reversal. He noted that no member of Congress, of the State Department or other high branches of government, no judge, no newspaper editor had yet confessed to being a Communist. How does this square with the knowledge that the Communist conspiracy has placed men in such positions to assure its aim of conquest? The conspiracy, he said, develops "men of steel" who will never show their true colors until the moment of takeover. He told his listeners that government units designed to combat the enemy, such as the Central Intelligence Agency, were overrun with infiltrators.

Hargis praised the lecture as a "masterpiece" which had provided the kind of information that should be put in book form for the students to take home and disseminate. In his own allusions to race, the evangelist came no closer to inciting his hearers than to assail Martin Luther King as a "phony" agitator. His writings, however, include such touches as "the *café-au-lait* statesmen" representing some of the newer members of the United Nations.

For the pocketbook-minded at the seminar, Mayor J. Bracken Lee of Salt Lake City and Captain Eddie Rickenbacker of Eastern Air Lines denounced the income tax as unnecessary. The government programs this revenue supports, they said, could be dropped. Foreign aid, the United Nations, and the maintenance of diplomatic relations with Communist and neutral nations also could be dispensed with, most faculty members agreed.

Mrs. Harry Artz Alexander of Grenada, Mississippi, described how to screen school textbooks for socialist propaganda. A minister from Midland, Texas, handed out reports to show that *Andersonville, Marjorie Morningstar,* and other books discovered in a school library there were subversive or obscene.

Ex-Communists on the faculty who make a living by writing exposés and speaking for fees, including Benjamin Gitlow, former head of the Party in this country, imparted their own special insight and were warmly received. One of them, Barbara Hartle, suggested that the way to tell if there were any liberals in a supposedly conservative audience was to conduct a pledge of allegiance to the flag and note whether anyone failed to participate.

M. G. Lowman, founder-director of Circuit Riders, Inc., of Cincinnati, which rides herd on clergymen and churches, brought the school up to date on "subversion" in religion. This was a subject of particular appeal because many of the students were fundamentalist ministers long chary of their brethren in the National Council of Churches. They were amply rewarded when Lowman "disclosed" that the National Council was, in part, a veritable hotbed of communism.

Representatives Scherer, who serves on the House Committee on Un-American Activities, and Rousselot made pleas for support of the conservative cause at the polls. Retired Major General Charles A. Willoughby, former intelligence chief for General Douglas MacArthur and now writer of a "foreign intelligence digest" for Billy James' *Weekly Crusader*, recalled espionage cases of the MacArthur era and sought to relate them to the present.

To potential "crusaders" whose interest is pricked by any of these appeals, Hargis repeats the reminder that Christian Crusade is a nonprofit, tax-exempt religious organization to which contributions are tax-free. Because of a lively interest in politics and in electing conservative politicians, the evangelist frequently skates close to the edge of legal tolerance. The Internal Revenue Code prohibits exempt organizations operated for religious purposes from devoting "any substantial part" of their activities to intervention "in any political campaign on behalf of any candidate for public office." This restriction applies to Christian Echoes National Ministry, Inc., the corporate name of Christian Crusade.

When Hargis discusses politics he seeks to dissociate his views from Christian Crusade. He puts on another hat, reserved for the occasion. He is a former president of We, the People!, another Right-wing group and one that has no religious, tax-exempt status. "When I want to engage in political action I can do it through We, the People!," he says.

One of Billy James' most cherished goals has been to bring about an effective coalition of leaders of the hundreds of Right-wing organizations, large and small, around the country. "These movements," he wrote, "in order to do the most effective job . . . must be indoctrinated, trained with facts and coordinated in their actions."

He said J. Edgar Hoover had appealed to these groups to adhere to facts and avoid generalities. "Christian Crusade today accepts the challenge of J. Edgar Hoover to properly indoctrinate the anti-Communist forces," he asserted.

Hargis' success in achieving unity of the Far Right has been meager. He called a meeting in Washington in 1962 to which he invited 350 Right-wing organizations. Members of seventy attended. The purpose was to establish formal contact with conservative congressmen. Hargis expected fifty legislators to attend. Only two showed up—Representatives Rousselot, since defeated, and E. Y. Berry, Republican of South Dakota. The Rightist coalition failed to materialize.

Hargis claims no real interest in either major political party. He could channel his support into one party, he said, only if Republicans and Democrats were realigned, as in England, into conservative and liberal parties. "We can no longer depend upon national political parties to rescue us from the decadence of liberalism, which the Communists exploit so expertly to their advantage," he says. "There must be a grass-roots conservative, pro-American, pro-Christian force that transcends political loyalties."

Hargis can hardly contain himself when it comes to discussing Walker. The evangelist says the retired general was "muzzled" for trying to teach his men patriotism. He calls him the "hero" of the incident. "Maj. Gen. Edwin A. Walker is a great man," Hargis has written, "a great American and the kind of a patriot that I pray God will give us in the White House. He stands with the Patrick Henry's, the Henry Clay's, the Abe Lincoln's. He is a champion of Americanism, a genuine statesman! Thank God for him and long may he live!"

At the request of Senator Strom Thurmond, Democrat of South Carolina, the Christian Crusade, the John Birch Society, and other groups solicited letters to Congress to demonstrate popular demand for a hearing in the "muzzling" case. Billy James got on the radio with an appeal. The result of the Right-wing organizations' effort, he said, was 147,000 letters in three days.

Hargis says he has no personal political ambitions. But he is eager to try to shape the political make-up of state and national legislative and administrative bodies by lending the weight of his influence where he has built it—with thousands of voters who listen to his advice on how to fight communism.

He also says that leading a return to nationalism calls for a man with a dynamic and inspirational personality. And he leaves the impression that he, being used for "a purpose," qualifies where no one else would.

He has a foolproof answer to charges of blending too much politics with religion. "Recently I have been accused by men in high circles of being too political," he wrote in 1962. "Only I can know the innermost motivations and desires of my heart."

6:

Searcy, Arkansas

In central Arkansas, not far from the foothills of the Ozarks, lies the peaceful little town of Searcy (pronounced *Sur'cy* by its 7200 residents). With its town square, lackluster shops, and leisurely pace, it seems indistinguishable from other sun-baked Southern towns. But Searcy is not exactly like any of them. It has Harding College, which has the National Education Program, which has made Searcy the academic seat of the Ultra Right.

Harding's National Education Program is and has been for many years one of the most aggressive organizations for ultraconservatism in the nation. Every year, a hundred thousand newspaper columns, newsletters, speech reprints, tapes, pamphlets, leaflets, flannelboard presentations, and anti-Communist study guides pour out of Harding's offices for use by newspapers, radio and television stations, businesses, schools, civic groups, and itinerant anti-Communist seminars. The Program consists of unending warnings of perils to the free-enterprise system to be found in communism, socialism, liberalism, and the views of politicians ideologically to the left of Senator Goldwater.

The president of the Program as well as principal proponent of its message is George Stuart Benson. When Benson returned from missionary service in China in 1936 to become president of Harding, which is operated by the fundamentalist Church of Christ, the college lacked three essentials: academic accreditation, an adequate campus (there were only two buildings), and a sufficient number of students (it had 200). Now Harding is a thriving conservative arts college with spacious grounds, modern buildings, and an enrollment of more than 1000.

The official regional accrediting agency was able to bestow its blessing on Harding in 1954 after the National Education Program was made a separate corporate entity. The affluent appearance of both college and Program, since 1953 a non-profit tax-free educational agency with substantial rent-free quarters on the campus, is attributable to the appeal of the Benson philosophy and the magic of Benson salesmanship to big business.

To say that once-struggling Harding College is now comfortably financed would be an understatement. The little institution's endowment fund, almost entirely from industrial donors, is about $6,000,000.

Benson scored his first smash hit with American industry in the late 1940s. Writing and speaking at a tireless pace, he built his message on the theme that unless business interests resold Americans on "the fundamentals of our way of life," the free-enterprise system would go down the drain.

For Benson, born in 1898, the danger appears to be the same that more recent entries in the business of anticommunism perceive. The United States is the last important bastion of resistance to godless, enslaving communism. The Communists are at our throats. Most of us are unaware of it, so insidious is their advance. Socialism, last step before communism, arrives in deceptive forms: medical aid to the aged, federal aid to education, rent controls, social security, foreign aid, liberalism in religion, growing power of organized labor.

One lecture reached Alfred P. Sloan, Jr., then board chairman of General Motors, in 1949; he was impressed enough to give Harding $300,000, which was used to start the National Education Program's later-considerable output of such motion pictures as "Communism on the Map." Industry took to this and other Program material, and Harding and Benson prospered.

"Communism on the Map" has been seen by millions of persons in industrial plants, schools, clubs, and on military bases. It is a professionally produced and narrated movie dramatizing the Communist takeovers in China, Czechoslovakia, Cuba, and other countries. Fidel Castro is depicted as triumphing over an "anti-Communist" Batista regime with the aid of the United States government. The Chinese Communists had similar help, the film hints, when the late General George C. Marshall represented Washington in effecting the crucial truce.

With a striking use of color, the entire world is shown turning pink and red. Only Spain and Switzerland hold out against the tide. The United States, red arrows encircling it menacingly, bears an ominous question mark at the climax.

The film has been widely condemned as purposely distorted. For example, ninety-two members of the faculty of the University of Washington wrote after a campus showing: "Having seen this film strip, we are shocked by its irresponsible mingling of fact and falsehood and by its gross distortion of historical events. As scholars, concerned with the truth, we protest against this harmful and misleading propaganda."

To which the white-haired, schoolmasterly president of the Program that produced it replies that these ninety-two were only 7 per cent of the Washington faculty, a mighty small percentage to question the veracity of his film.

The Pentagon agreed with the assessment of the 7 per cent and others and removed it from its list of approved educational tools after military commanders had been making considerable use of the movie in troop information and education programs. It remains a favorite at gatherings of extremist organizations. Robert Welch gives the Birch Society credit for tens of thousands of showings.

The feeling of mutuality between Benson and Birchers is strong. Benson has said: "Any American who loves freedom and is willing to work, work, work to protect it can find intelligent direction and companionship in a John Birch Society group."

The producer of "Communism on the Map," Glenn A. Green, a Bircher, has since left Searcy to join the National Right to Work Committee. Meanwhile, the National Education Program has updated the movie with new ones called "Communist Encirclement" and "Communism in Action." These films and others can be purchased or rented.

Besides movies, one of the most popular items in the Program portfolio, as far as industry is concerned, is the "Freedom Forum." Harding offers these "Forums," with speakers, films, and literature, anywhere in the country. They vary in length of presentation from one to several days. Some plants have made such presentations available to their employees on company time and on a compulsory basis.

In addition to the Harding exports, five-day forums are held annually on the campus. Attendance fees range up to $140. It is the stated purpose of these forums "to refresh those attending with the fundamental facts about our American capitalism and the forces now seeking its destruction . . . and to stimulate conferees to return to their respective organizations and communities and become leaders of resistance to the spread of Socialism and Communism."

Speakers have included Benson, Schwarz, Skousen, Manion, Fred W. Hartley, and retired General Albert C. Wedemeyer. Representatives of at least a thousand companies have attended. The forums draw goodly numbers of clergymen and school officials as well as people from industry. Some concerns also send molders of opinion in their communities. A teacher sponsored by a Milwaukee company expressed his thanks as follows:

The Freedom Forum in its entirety was the most intense and enlightening week of education I have ever experienced. It has had a profound effect on my thinking relative to the liberal climate now too prevalent in our great country. I have a better and more appreciative understanding of the free enterprise or capitalistic system as we know it. You might say I have become a disciple of the virtues of private property, the profit motive and constitutional government where before I was only a passive follower of our American way of life.

The communistic threat was portrayed so clearly to me I shudder at the thought of its motives and its success to date. I now clearly see that socialism and the welfare state are the worms that gnaw at the pillars of what account for America's high standard of living. . . .

I learned more clearly that labor bosses today have usurped the laborer of his constitutional rights and these labor leaders must be curbed lest we find they completely dominate the American scene to the detriment of all freedom loving Americans. Mr. Hartley of Taft-Hartley very thoroughly explained the sins of mass picketing, secondary boycotts, the criminal element in unionism and union leadership with political aspirations. . . .

I have begun to disseminate the acquired knowledge to my class of graduating eighth graders, to teachers I associate with, to people in my church and with a vigor

I hope will inspire the listener to become a disciple in the crucial battle now being waged on all fronts against our American system.

I hope in the future I will prove worthy of the expense and confidence you and the Nordberg Manufacturing Company had in sending me. If ever this educator can cooperate with free enterprise I am your willing partner.

With such results, corporations of all sizes have lined up to provide tax-deductible financial backing for the National Education Program.

Another Program program involves study outlines for history, government, and economics courses. These outlines, for high schools, are designed to imbue students with a solidly conservative point of view.

"We've said for fifteen years we were going to stop communism," Benson said in a chat at Searcy's College Church of Christ before going in to teach his Sunday School class. "We haven't. Government policies will be altered only when the public demands it."

He said the public demand for godliness and patriotism could be fashioned "through teaching alone." To this end the Program has prepared course outlines suggesting textbooks, reference books, pamphlets, tape recordings, speeches, and audio-visual aids teachers should use. Recommended authors include Benson, J. B. Matthews, Schwarz, Philbrick, former Senator William E. Jenner of Indiana, and Arens.

The outlines, provided free to any teacher who expresses an interest in them, were being used in more than 300 schools around the country in 1962. Revisions arrive from Searcy as "better material" turns up. Some schools prepare their own outlines for teaching Americanism. Harding's study guides, a Program brochure says, have aided "several hundred" such school systems "in the establishment of sound courses."

The guide for teaching American history, for example, lists "an understanding and appreciation of the Republican form of government, as contrasted with pure democracy and various types of Socialism" as a goal to be developed in each student. Another goal is a "sense of patriotism inspiring a desire and a determination to work toward building a better nation while protecting its basic structure from all forces which might destroy it." In the American economics teaching guide, a goal to be developed in students is "knowledge and understanding that planning begins with isolated interferences with the free economy and ends as the controlling mechanism of the authoritarian state."

Representatives of the Program promote interest by traveling about the country speaking to educators and addressing Parent-Teacher Associations and civic groups.

Harding's National Education Program turns out still other items for its school kit. A series of Hollywood-produced cartoons extolling rugged individualism and self-reliance as the American way have been distributed to thousands of schools in recent years. "Supplemental textual materials" designed to "strengthen and safeguard the structure of American freedom" are made available. Some school districts are reported to have put thousands of dollars into such Program materials.

The Program, budgeted at $200,000 a year, sent staff members to Europe to select information for a series of film strips designed to show how wage earners fare under capitalism compared with "Welfare State Socialism." The resulting half-dozen strips "document" shortcomings abroad "in dramatic detail," a Program booklet says. Distribution of the strips began in 1959 through friends of Harding in industry, education, the American Farm Bureau Federation, and community groups.

The Program's views also reach millions through the printed word. Benson writes a weekly column, "Looking Ahead," that is mailed free to 3200 newspapers (largely weeklies) and other publications. These columns cover every subject that raises the blood pressure of the Far Right. Here is a typical sampling of opening paragraphs:

> In the opinion of some of the best informed and most respected legal minds in our nation, one of the gravest dangers to our traditional American way of life and all the great blessings it has made possible for generations of Americans, is the present seeming determination of the United States Supreme Court to break away from its historic function and become a maker of laws and a destroyer of laws to suit the whims of its nine justices.

> There has just come to my attention a highly professional analysis of sociology textbooks which should be read by every good teacher, college professor and parent in America. It brings to light shocking facts about some textbooks now used in high schools and colleges in the country.

> A recent nationwide sampling of high school seniors revealed that 55 per cent knew so little or cared so little about the economic system under which we live that they agreed with the keystone Communist doctrine of "from each according to his ability, to each according to his need."

The conclusions to which these introductions lead match those of the rest of the Right-wing fraternity on the same subjects. An abbreviated column called "Listen Americans!" is sent without charge to about a thousand business concerns for their house organs.

In addition, a "National Program Letter" is sent monthly to some 50,000 "thought leaders" who subscribe at $1 a year. Bulk lots of reprints can be ordered at reduced rates by companies to stuff pay envelopes or for reading racks and reception rooms.

Besides grinding out its message in these many ways, the

articulate top command of Harding and Program crisscross the country to fill lecture engagements. Led by their indefatigable president, they constitute a six-man speaker's bureau on call at all times to hop on a plane and deliver the Program's message to interested organizations. With the proliferation of groups on the Far Right, the speaker's bureau has been in constant demand.

The admiration of businessmen for the Harding program is based in large measure on economic self-interest. Harding is an unremitting fountainhead of "free enterprise" publicity: the cost of government is growing at an alarming rate, excessive taxes on industry reduce incentive to produce, states must pass and enforce "right-to-work" laws to keep employees out of the clutches of Big Labor.

Alan F. Westin, associate professor of public law and government at Columbia University, estimated, on the basis of surveys of annual corporate donations and published records of gifts of companies to Right-wing organizations, that the business community contributed about $10,000,000 to the Radical Right in 1961.

Benson pursues his course with zeal. Besides his administrative responsibilities, writing chores, and church work, he averages 140 speeches annually. As early as 1948, Harding took the precaution of insuring his life for a million dollars. He was then laboring at the height of his capacity to save the country, and he has not diminished the pace since. In fact, he has hardly wasted a moment since he left his father's Oklahoma farm. If the country goes "socialist," it won't be the fault of George S. Benson, Harding College, or the National Education Program of tiny, sunny Searcy, Arkansas.

7:

Kent and Phoebe

Post office boxes 4223 and 4254, New Orleans 18, Louisiana, are the addresses for one of the most energetic operations of the Far Right. They are the mail drops for Kent and Phoebe Courtney, who operate out of shabby quarters in a clapboard store at 7819 Green Street and an old wooden bungalow a few blocks away on Pine Street.

At the Green Street address a dusty Venetian blind hangs in the window behind a display card that offers to print wedding invitations "just like Miss America's." A sign identifies the establishment as the Pelican Printing Company. Inside, the activity is far more complex than the front would hint. This is the Courtneys' production center.

Sixty thousand dollars' worth of modern offset printing equipment is kept busy turning out many different publications: a quarter-a-copy "newspaper" called *Independent American* that is published every month or so; a series of bulletins called "Tax Fax"; propaganda for the establishment of a national Right-wing political party through the Courtneys' Conservative Society of America; an ultraconservative index of the voting records of congressmen; a paperback volume entitled *The Case of General Edwin A. Walker: A documented exposé: How the Appeasers Propose to Substitute Surrender for Victory.*

Courtney, a red-haired, 240-pound man, and his wife Phoebe, a strapping woman who wears her graying hair in a coil on top of her head, put their gross take in 1961 from all sources, including speaking fees and contributions, at $150,000.

The Courtneys employ fifteen printers, mailers, and researchers. In 1961 they sent out more than 950,000 pieces of mail, including one that they claim helped stymie in the Senate the President's request for a Department of Urban Affairs.

Forty thousand copies of a twelve-page pamphlet entitled "Kennedy's Power Grab: The Department of Urban Affairs—A blueprint for the destruction of private property and States' rights," went out in the three weeks before the bill was presented to the Senate. The pamphlet asserted that ". . . the Urban Renewal Program jeopardizes the right to own and hold private property. Significantly, the abolition of the right to own private property is one of the goals set forth in the Communist Manifesto."

The Courtneys say that at least 30,000 copies of the pamphlets were mailed to congressmen by individuals around the country. One banker in Memphis, they say, bought thousands of them and included one with every monthly statement sent out.

The pamphlet business is the biggest part of the operation. Although Kent Courtney is secretive about the names of corporations that buy his "Tax Fax" flyers—sample titles: "The Income Tax Can Be Repealed," "Impeach Earl Warren?," "Rockefeller Now Controls U.S. Foreign Policy"—he says that several large companies, including a soft-drink bottler in California and a major aircraft manufacturer, buy them in bulk and put them into employees' pay envelopes. Every sale also is pay in his own envelope, the key objective of the Courtney enterprises.

Courtney was born in St. Paul, Minnesota, in 1918. After an uneventful childhood in New Orleans, he finished his studies at Tulane University in time to serve in World War II, first in the Navy, then as a contract pilot for the Air Transport Command. In the early postwar years he flew as a commercial pilot. Then he taught market research, economics, money and banking, and history of American business at a Tulane evening school.

In 1955 he became an entrepreneur of the Far Right by starting publication of the *Independent American*. He claims 15,000 subscribers to the paper, edited by Phoebe. Russell Kirk calls it a "hate sheet." The pages are crammed with editorial comment from the most reactionary segment of the nation's press. Much of the advertising is for the Courtneys' own printed products.

Courtney also has a weekly radio program in which he bills himself as "Kent Courtney, News Analyst." The program, called the "Radio Edition of the *Independent American*," is broadcast by about thirty-five independent stations. His commentary consists of slam-bang attacks that echo his pamphlets and his newspaper.

Courtney says he believes the only effective way to halt Communist subversion and takeover is through political action. In recent years he has devoted much of his considerable energy to efforts to form a third party to take on the Republicans and Democrats. Neither major party offers any hope for conservatives, he says. Late in 1962 the *Independent American* offered "final proof that the Communist-accommodating Council on Foreign Relations now controls both the Democrat and the Republican parties."

"A *new party* is the only hope for this nation," it said.

An epilogue in the Walker book pointed out that "there

are hundreds of anti-Communist educational groups and study clubs active throughout the United States, and the number is increasing by the week."

"Some operate on a local basis," it said, "some on a state basis, while others are national in scope. The purpose of these organizations is to educate their members and the American public concerning the menace of the Communist conspiracy at home and abroad. For various reasons, such as tax deductibility, these anti-Communist groups must limit their activities to education of the threat of Communism, and are not able to extend their activities into the field of political action or politics." Others that are not so circumscribed are nevertheless interested only in certain issues, such as repeal of the income tax.

To fill the void and push his third-party ambitions, Courtney organized the Conservative Society of America in 1961. He says it is not a political party but could become the nucleus of one. He has sought to make the political-action group appeal to both militant anti-Communists and racial segregationists. It was organized, he said at the time of the riot-scarred enrollment of the first Negro at the University of Mississippi, because there was no political party to represent "those who resist the Federal encroachment in areas of education historically reserved to the states" or "those who wish to defend the national sovereignty of the United States from external aggression."

In his "research headquarters" he has a map dotted with place pins that show the strength of the organization. He claims members, at $20 a year, in forty-six states. Greatest strength is in California, where, even according to Courtney, "political fads have had a good history."

The Society's letterhead lists Courtney as chairman. Seventeen others, familiar in Far Right circles, also are on the list. It includes Willoughby, Lee, and Medford Evans, Sr., one of Robert Welch's original Birch organizers.

The Society publishes a voting index by which constituents can gauge the conservatism of their congressmen on specified issues. In addition, the *Independent American* offered a guide to voting in the November 1962 election. Until a third party is functioning, the Courtneys believe, the only effective way to fight Communist appeasement in government is to support conservatives of existing parties at the polls. To this end, they advocated election of candidates in such terms as these: James D. Martin, Alabama Republican, "opposing 100 per cent pro-Socialist Sen. Lister Hill"; Dr. Kenneth Jones, Arkansas Republican, "opposing ultra-Liberal, 75 per cent pro-Socialist Sen. J. William Fulbright"; Dr. Daniel Beltz, California Republican, "opposing extreme Leftist, 100 per cent pro-Socialist Rep. James Roosevelt"; David C. Treen, Louisiana Republican, "opposing Kennedy's rubber stamp Democratic incumbent, Rep. Hale Boggs"; Kieran O'Doherty, New York Conservative, "opposing Left-Wing Internationalist, 92 per cent pro-Socialist Jacob K. Javits" for the Senate. The percentages were derived from a Courtney analysis of incumbents' voting records. The Courtney endorsements produced no upsets.

Courtney has waded into politics personally time and again, each time scoring a whopping failure. He has alienated Goldwater, Kirk, and others of the Respectable Right. But pamphleteering provides the necessary money and discouragement comes hard. He plans to run for governor under the States' Rights Party banner again. "After all," he says, "you're nobody in Louisiana politics until you've been beaten in gubernatorial campaigns at least three or four times."

Courtney helped organize T. Coleman Andrews' States' Rights Party in 1956 and worked to get the candidate on the ballot in seventeen states.

In 1959, before the general public had heard of Robert Welch and the John Birch Society, Courtney had him as a speaker, along with William Buckley, at a rally in Chicago to organize a coalition of patriotic and conservative groups into a "New Party." The effort quickly fell through. Welch described the meeting as "an unauthorized rally in support of Barry Goldwater" and told his audience that he was against a third party but for the nomination of Goldwater as the Republican presidential candidate. Welch took pains to point out that nothing he said had been cleared by the Senator, who in fact had disowned the entire rally.

Despite the rebuff, just before the 1960 Republican convention in Chicago Courtney sought to organize a "Goldwater for President" publicity blitz. Armed with a delegate's floor badge he says he "got from a friend," he descended on the convention. In his New Orleans print shop he had prepared scores of "Goldwater for President" placards. With the aid of friends, he sent placard-waving troops into the field: "I told them to push those signs into the lens of every television camera they saw." Soon, Courtney claims, he had control of an organization of "Youth for Goldwater" enthusiasts, had them scratching the *Vice* from posters backing the Senator for Vice-President, and had volunteers parading up and down Michigan Avenue. Whenever he got word that Goldwater was about to enter or leave the convention amphitheater or a hotel, Courtney called signals and a detachment of sign-shaking youngsters rushed to the scene.

But the Senator from Arizona remained aloof. Courtney says that Goldwater would have no part of his activities and that he never even managed to discuss the matter with the Senator. Later Goldwater completely disavowed any support he might be getting from the fat man from New Orleans. Finally, after the convention had nominated Richard Nixon and Goldwater had pledged his support, Courtney's adoration of the Arizonan turned to suspicion. "Tax Fax" pamphlet No. 32, "Is Goldwater Really a Conservative?," charged that "Goldwater is watering down his views in the face of Rockefeller's aggressiveness."

The Courtneys later said Goldwater was "a Judas goat, collecting conservative dough as chairman of the GOP Senate Campaign Committee to help elect liberal-socialists like Javits of New York." Phoebe turns pale when she is asked about Goldwater. "If he wrote that book [*Conscience of a Conservative*] again in his own blood I wouldn't believe him," she says. "I don't trust him. I'd never accept him as a candidate." Her husband says he has been "tainted by socialism."

In 1961 the Courtneys held another rally in Chicago. Welch wished them well but declined to come. In *American Opinion*, he explained that ". . . Kent Courtney is trying to fight this whole battle on the political front and through political means, and therefore he actually needs and seeks publicity; while we are fighting on an educational front, and all of this publicity is the last thing we wanted. Also, Kent believes that the proper approach politically is through a Third Party. We neither endorse nor oppose a Third Party— at least at this time—primarily because we take no direct part in politics."

Next the Courtneys sought to promote Walker for high political office. This ended when the retired general ran last in a field of six in the 1962 Texas Democratic gubernatorial primary.

Courtney's hit-and miss flailing about on the Far Right has frequently left him spinning awkwardly there, successful in the collection of money from undiscriminating fanciers of pamphlets, but completely ineffectual in his batterings on the door of American politics.

8:
The National Indignation Convention

"Indignation, Texas Style." This was the way the first meeting in Dallas of the new fire-eating group was billed in the fall of 1961, and it lived up to its advances. One man's indignation spread to a second, then to thousands of others, and hardened into a new organization of the Far Right. Its goal, carried to completion, would have been impeachment of the President and dismissal of his Cabinet. The men who stirred public indignation and then organized it demanded that everyone be fired—in or out of the White House, the State Department, the military services, or the Congress—who had anything to do with the sale of surplus fighter planes to Yugoslavia and the training of Tito's pilots to fly them. Expression of violent opposition to the sale of surplus Saberjets to Communist Yugoslavia served as the opening fusillade for an emotionally charged organization that mushroomed under the name *National Indignation Convention*.

The movement originated with a letter of protest, written on September 27, 1961, by Harry E. Knickerbocker, Jr., a major in Texas' Air National Guard. The young Dallas insurance man had gone to Perrin Air Force Base near Sherman, Texas, to see about some equipment for his unit. When he returned to Dallas he wrote to Senator Tower:

> As an Air National Guard pilot, I had occasion to visit Perrin Air Force Base, Sherman, Texas, seeking some ground training equipment for our 136th Fighter Group (AD) in Dallas, equipment that will soon be declared excess to Air Force needs.
>
> I found the equipment I sought, but I found something else far more important: COMMUNIST pilots are receiving training in the USAF F–86L interceptor course at Perrin Air Force Base.
>
> Yugoslav Captains Rizman, Lukie, and Cunzaric were on the flight lines along with trainees from our ally nations ... West Germans, Free Chinese, etc. receiving briefing from American instructors. I was told that a fourth Communist pilot is also in training, but I did not see or talk with him during my visit.
>
> When asked how they feel about training COMMUNIST pilots, the American instructors usually shrugged, grinned and suggested that it was not best to question such things.
>
> German pilots in training at Perrin are less reticent. They say, "THESE COMMUNISTS ARE THE PILOTS WE ARE GOING TO HAVE TO FIGHT. WHY ARE YOU TRAINING THEM ALONGSIDE YOUR ALLIES?" I couldn't give a reasonable answer to this question. Can you, Senator?
>
> The training of YUGOSLAVS at an American Air Force Base may be glibly explained away by our State Department as AID to "neutral" countries but such an explanation would be simply too much for me to swallow.

COMMUNISTS . . . ALL communists, regardless of nationality . . . are ENEMIES OF AMERICA. Training America's enemies constitutes giving aid and comfort to them. Giving aid and comfort to America's enemies is defined in Article 3, Section 3 of the CONSTITUTION as TREASON. Any way you add it up, you reach the same result.

It may be said that those responsible for this act sincerely believed themselves to be acting in the best interests of America. Benedict Arnold's biography reveals that up to the moment he defected to the British, he was one of America's staunchest patriots. Furthermore, Arnold felt that by achieving a quick end of the bloodshed and awful suffering that characterized what he believed to be a lost cause, he would serve his fellow Americans best.

Benedict Arnold was sincere in his belief but he will be remembered always (I hope) as the symbol of American TREASON. Modern traitors, whoever they may be, however high their offices and however sincere they may be . . . ARE STILL TRAITORS! No amount of sincerity can change that. Their acts must not be excused and they must not go unpunished.

In view of the unprecedented reprimand of a patriot of the magnitude of General Walker it seems likely that revelation of these facts will do little to further my individual progress as an officer in The Air National Guard. It is obvious that today the multiple criminality of Communism is honored above GOD-fearing American patriotism. Nevertheless, I for one, official Defense Department policy notwithstanding, can serve only ONE master. I remain an unreconstructed, unliberalized, unsocialized, uncommunized American.

Rest assured I will support any action you deem appropriate to rectify the treasonous situation herein described.

Major Knickerbocker had a legitimate complaint. Although he was not aware of it, the same complaint had been made in Congress. Senator Tower promised to look into it further. Meanwhile, on October 13, 1961, the Dallas *News* printed Knickerbocker's letter and let out an editorial shriek. One of the readers of both letter and editorial was Frank McGehee, a tall, curly-haired Dallas garage owner and Korean War fighter pilot. Furious, he decided to do something about it.

McGehee, a member of the Birch Society, called a few friends and raised several hundred dollars. With it he rented the Dallas Memorial Auditorium for an "indignation" meeting. Dallas radio stations, meanwhile, were telling of plans to get up an Indignation Motorcade to demonstrate at Perrin. Some thirty-six hours after the letter appeared in the paper, an auto caravan left Dallas for the air base. Police barred its entry and the Indignants settled for picketing at the gates.

But there was action in Dallas. People piled into the Auditorium, sometimes used as a wrestling arena, in a fighting mood. McGehee wanted to telephone President Kennedy and Vice-President Johnson and ask them to talk to the crowd over a loudspeaker hookup, but thought better of it and started calling Texas congressmen. "We decided that to get this thing rolling we'll have to start on a smaller scale," he told reporters that night, "so that the movement won't be stopped in the higher levels of Washington."

That first night 200 people were in the hall. A thousand were on hand the second night. By the third session there were 1500, some of them women who came carrying babies or leading older children.

"The United States is training Red Yugoslav aviators at Perrin Air Force Base right here in Texas!" shouted the 220-lb. McGehee. His face colored. "Now let's figure out what to do about this. As for me, I wouldn't give my enemy a bow and arrow."

The original Indignant, Major Knickerbocker, stood on the edge of the stage and declared: "The State Department says the planes the Red pilots are flying are obsolete, and then the government gives them to the Air National Guard to fly. The State Department says the program is all right because it's been going on for seven years. Murder has been going for longer than that."

The crowd yelled its approval. McGehee then asked for come help in paying for the hall, and money floated down from the balconies. Pretty girls carrying baskets picked it up and moved through the audience to collect more.

When the three nights of organized anger were over, the National Indignation Convention had been born. Within days after the first sessions were held in Dallas, meetings based on McGehee's pattern of protest had been held throughout the South. McGehee invited delegates of these other conventions to a meeting in Dallas where the "indignants" could organize into a national body. In November 1961, some 2400 delegates showed up for the three-day affair. It was quite a show, even for Dallas.

The stage of the Auditorium sported a bank of telephones, all tied into loudspeakers so the audience, if it would stay quiet long enough, could hear the conversation. McGehee busily placed calls to congressmen, asking that they explain the program of military aid to Yugoslavia.

Between calls, McGehee and others held forth at the microphone. Thomas J. Anderson, publisher of *Farm and Ranch* and a member of the Birch Society's National Council, had come from Nashville. Also present was a home-grown patriot familiar to Texans, rancher J. Evetts Haley. At one point in the proceedings of the first session, Anderson, at the microphone, spotted the Texan and beckoned him to the stage. He introduced Haley as a man "who's been in this fight for twenty years."

"Tom Anderson must be turning moderate," the wealthy

rancher responded. "He only wants to impeach Earl Warren. I'd hang him."

The house rang with applause.

Haley had handled audiences like this one before. The wealthy cattleman is the chief of Texans for America, an organization devoted to keeping "subversive textbooks" out of the hands of school children. In 1961 the group managed to have more than fifty books removed from Texas schools.

While Haley held the microphone, Captain Eddie Rickenbacker came in on the phone to address the convention. He told the Indignants that some day the American people would realize their mistakes and "erect a monument to Joe McCarthy." He had no word on the planes-for-Tito issue, but his stand was known. When the Miami mechanics of his airline had walked off the job because Yugoslavs were visiting, Rickenbacker had called the local union leader to say that he approved.

Though not known to be a member of any of the major Far Right organizations, Rickenbacker is viewed by many as an elder statesman of the movement. His pleas usually call for a return to the "old-fashioned patriotism" and individualism that he says would be served by abolishing the income tax, withdrawing from the UN, breaking relations with the Soviet Union and the neutral nations, and using the big stick.

When Rickenbacker finished, McGehee shouted, "Who do you want to talk to now?" The not-in-unison audience responded, "The President, the Vice-President, Rusk" and the names of half a dozen congressmen.

For those congressmen who came to the phone McGehee had three questions:

> Why haven't all military men from Communist countries receiving aid or training in the United States been deported?
> Why haven't all contracts calling for the sale of military

equipment, current or obsolete, to Communist countries been canceled?

What are the names of the people responsible for this program and why haven't they been fired?

Congressmen reminded the meeting that the arrangements for the sale of obsolete military equipment to Yugoslavia had been made under the Eisenhower administration and approved by Congress. They also offered the cold-war political reasons for support of Tito. But their explanations failed to impress the men and women in the Indignation Auditorium.

Representative Bruce Alger, Dallas Republican ranked high in the Courtney index, told the meeting, "I will be your voice in Washington."

McGehee did not seek to exercise strict control over the movement. "All I can do," he said, "is make suggestions. Anybody can put on an indignation convention." Quite a few did, channeling wrath aroused first by planes for Tito. Other targets included desegregation, income tax, fluoridation, the United Nations.

But at all the early indignation conventions there was general agreement that a resolution should be adopted by Congress that would stop military training of Communists in the United States, forbid transfer of aircraft or other weapons to Communist countries, and remove from office any government official found guilty of violating the resolution's provisions. Such a resolution was introduced in the Senate in 1962 by Tower and in the House by Alger and Rousselot.

By then some 200 conventions had been held in cities across the country, primarily in the Deep South, and the National Indignation Convention had "continuity centers" in twenty-five cities, plus 700 committees in 200 congressional districts in thirty-four states. It had grown faster and more noisily than anything else on the Far Right. McGehee had to give up the garage business to work at his new job full time in offices rented in downtown Dallas, drawing a salary of $175 a week when contributions were adequate to pay it.

Sale of planes to Yugoslavia and training of Yugoslav pilots ended quietly but abruptly, no doubt at least in part as a result of the furor raised by the new group. Congress passed a foreign-aid bill prohibiting aid to Communist countries unless the President found it vital to U.S. security. In the followup measure appropriating funds, the President's discretionary power was limited to economic aid; military aid was banned.

With the battle decided, the Tower and Alger resolutions were never pressed to a vote. Lacking any further issues beyond the clichés already overworked by established Rightist groups, the National Indignation Convention quickly faded from nationwide attention. A "national" gathering in Arlington, Virginia, in 1962 drew about seventy persons. The slam and fire and righteous indignation of the early meetings in Dallas were gone. Interest evaporated with the successful conclusion of the Yugoslav affair.

9:

The Minutemen

The new arrival—a slender, dark, handsome, well-dressed man—was surrounded by reporters who had seen his name tag. His appearance at the Mayo Hotel in Tulsa for a five-day anti-Communist meeting was unheralded. As national leader of the undercover Minutemen, he had been often spoken of but seldom seen at public meetings. Even Billy James Hargis, promoter of the "Anti-Communist Leadership Training School" at the hotel, had never met the quiet Missourian.

Robert Bolivar DePugh hardly presented a picture to match his reputation as the nation's farthest-out Right-winger. He was attentive to the proceedings, friendly, a bit shy. He was never recognized from the platform of the seminar. And though not shunned, neither was he part of the group throughout the week-long meeting.

The young drug manufacturer, a 180-pound six-footer who was thirty-eight years old at the time, said he was at the meeting to find out whether he could learn more about Communist techniques. Privately and with articulate candor he explained just what his organization planned to do to stave off the enemy if all else failed.

116

The Minutemen, a loose federation of small bands of men and women scattered throughout the country, are principally concerned with training themselves for guerrilla warfare. After the Communist takeover, they will deploy over hill and dale, dig in, and repulse with small arms any effort to enslave them.

The next objective will be to wax strong, recapture the United States or whatever it has been called under communism, and restore the "Constitutional Republic," freedom, and liberty.

The derision with which the nation, including fellow radicals Welch and Hargis, have greeted this program has neither deterred nor embittered DePugh. "I think almost everyone's opinion of us changes when they learn the facts about us," he says.

DePugh lives with his wife and five children in a modest frame home in the small town of Norborne, Missouri. He moved his drug concern there from Independence, Missouri, where he grew up. He learned his trade by working for other pharmaceutical companies after studying at Washburn and Kansas State universities and the University of Missouri. He served in the Coast Artillery during World War II.

The Minutemen grew out of a duck-hunting outing taken by DePugh and nine friends in 1959. They discussed how poorly prepared people would be if faced with the need for outdoor survival. They decided they would remedy this sad state, at least for themselves, by becoming a self-sufficient guerrilla band.

For two years they read and trained and expanded almost unnoticed, sharing their ideas with other groups that felt the call to self-preservation. The original ten constituted themselves as an Executive Committee to make policy and to encourage others to face up to reality with them.

The principal policy decision was to decide very little. Units were not to be closely bound to each other because it was in the nature of guerrilla warfare to operate independently. Once the Communists came, it might be every band for itself.

Secrecy of membership was maintained, even from the leadership, to insure against capture of files by the enemy. Even three years after the duck hunt, DePugh's only liaison with his troops was through the Executive Committee and two dozen "regional coordinators." He says, "I don't even know the members' names. All we ask is the name and address of the unit leader, and this can be a pseudonym."

The ten leaders scattered in time but maintained their roles. They and some 500 select members have been the sole financial support of the Minutemen's national headquarters operation. They contribute the $2000 to $3000 needed monthly for printing and mailing manuals and other material, DePugh says. He estimates that there may be a total of 25,000 Minutemen in the nation. Dues are "optional"—for most members whatever they want to contribute to the needs of their own five- to fifteen-man band.

"Each band must take care of its own finances," DePugh says. He explains that the Minutemen couldn't try to make a profit, as other Far Right organizations do, even if they wanted to. The reason: one of the greatest risks to the secrecy of the organization would be to have the Internal Revenue Service "pussyfooting around." "Sometimes it is harder to hide what you're doing from them than from the FBI or the NKVD," DePugh said.

Nationwide publicity burst upon the Minutemen, comfortably unknown till then, in 1961. In Shiloh, Illinois, authorities received complaints that some people were "playing with guns" at the Community Center. The sheriff investigated and found a unit of Minutemen holding a tactical seminar. He confiscated rifles, a burp gun, and a .30-caliber light machine gun, but charges of illegal possession of weapons later were dismissed. The seminar had included maneuvers in which DePugh and his wife, Romona Van, and a small group of assorted gun-toting Minutemen, some in camouflage suits and steel helmets, had been locked in bush-to-bush combat with an imaginary enemy.

Because one of the leaders was a firearms dealer, the exercise was well supported with weapons, which ranged from Browning automatics and smoke grenades to .81-millimeter mortars. Practice in marksmanship was combined with stream-fording and a practical workout in hit-and-dash-for-cover tactics.

About the same time, another nondescript band demonstrated in southern California the Minutemen's self-reliance when deprived of guns. For two days a group of San Diego men lived in the Anza Desert State Park on whatever they could find: coffee made of mesquite beans, boiled caterpillars, cactus wrens, lizards. Thus sustained, they prepared for any future brush with the enemy by tossing homemade grenades as they maneuvered at the ready over sand and cliff.

The flurry of publicity has made DePugh a "dead duck"— a marked man if the Reds come, he says. But it has also served as a lesson: the Minutemen now take care to cover their tracks.

"We still hold maneuvers all the time," he said in 1962, "but we make it a studied habit to leave no trace."

Minutemen bury or pocket used matches and everything else when they break camp. Not a tin can that might reflect light is left. In addition to maneuvers, most bands hold weekly meetings indoors, DePugh says. Manuals prepared from DePugh's library of some 300 books on guerrilla tactics are studied. Thirty-two-hour courses in guerrilla warfare have been issued. The authorities being studied include Mao Tse-tung and Ernesto "Che" Guevara. DePugh points out that Guevara and Fidel Castro operated a successful underground movement for a long time before their triumph in

Cuba, and so did the patriots of Denmark and Norway during World War II.

Meetings are disguised. "Security officers" are posted. If a visitor arrives at a house where Minutemen are at work, the meeting quickly becomes a poker game or some other form of social gathering. The number of cars parked in front of a meeting house is limited to avert suspicion, even if it forces some members to walk several blocks to attend.

"We have men who have eluded the Gestapo for years," DePugh said.

What does this incipient "underground" do at its meetings besides play poker and read Mao in preparation for maneuvers? Like its brother organizations of the Radical Right, it fights communism by alerting the nation to the evils thereof.

If the Minutemen limited themselves to kaffee klatches and beating the bramble they might reasonably expect to be labeled harmless oddities and left to their own devices. But, as DePugh points out, this is a nationwide effort to recruit and train an underground movement committed to saving America. Men and women with no intention of becoming guerrilla fighters are solicited as urgently as their hardier brethren. A primary indoors function is to distribute the literature of the Far Right, some of the most alarming of which is produced by the Minutemen themselves.

One pamphlet describes how Communists infiltrate government departments, then asks: "What do you really know about the Congressman from your district? The State Senator or the State Representative? Could any of these men have been indoctrinated in Communist ideology at some time in their career?

"We must be willing to continue the fight for liberty even though we no longer have the legal support of established authority and prepare ourselves to take any action—no matter how brutal—that may be required to renew the protection of the United States Constitution for future generations.

"We must investigate, by means of our own secret memberships, the possible infiltration of Communist sympathizers into American organizations of government, business, labor, religion or education."

DePugh lists such intelligence operations as one of the most important functions of the organization. He attended the Hargis seminar solely to seek new ideas and methods on how to proceed. "We're not trying to compete with the FBI or C.I.A.," he says. "But we feel we're in a better position to know our friends and neighbors than anybody else."

Putting the knowledge to use, Minutemen keep files on citizens they suspect. Without opening it for examination, one group leader showed a reporter his card index, containing names, addresses, and phone numbers of persons whose patriotism he doubted.

The Minutemen practice with "security checks" on their own members. Anybody interested in joining is admitted to the organization, but the code calls for a period of scrutiny and a thorough check on background before advancement to a position of responsibility.

"Indoor" members, mostly wives of the amateur militia men, undertook another check, a nationwide study of the suitability of school books in current use. They dropped the project when they found they were duplicating the work of other Right-wing organizations such as America's Future.

DePugh says the Minutemen have set up supply companies to stock gas masks, medicine, compasses, and other survival equipment against the day of reckoning. Some units have cached food and ammunition in the mountains. The supply companies will buy in volume ("such as 10,000 compasses in a single order," DePugh suggests) in order to get a good rate for resale to members.

Some things the Minutemen will produce for themselves,

such as inexpensive "Minute masks" chemically treated for protection from any Russian use of nerve gas and bacteriological warfare.

If, despite all these precautions, the supplies are by chance confiscated, well-trained Minutemen will not despair. The day will come, DePugh believes, when they will be able to start from scratch, as he says the Chinese managed to do after they were invaded by Japan in World War II, and provide for their every need, including firearms.

"If you left me naked in the desert," he says, "I could make gunpowder." The Minuteman formula for this is secret, but one potential ingredient, DePugh says, is the nitrate in human urine. A Minuteman handbook lists 1000 sources of explosives, he says.

Not every Minuteman's forte is chemistry, but each can make a contribution based on his trade, hobbies, or sheer ingenuity. Printers, for example, can counterfeit travel permits; weavers can make clothing. If the underground grows enough to demand it, mobile factories can be established, à la China again, to move with and supply the troops from hideout to hideout.

The need for Minutemen to make their own firearms could arise before the Communist takeover, DePugh explains, if the government should abridge the constitutional guarantee of the right to bear arms. The soft-spoken guerrilla said, with his trace of twang, that his organization was preparing for this eventuality.

Minutemen meetings that display and study small arms generally do not violate the law, although state laws differ. DePugh notes that some states prohibit parading and maneuvering with arms but do not enforce the regulation because even an American Legion parade would be a violation.

There is a federal statute against raising a private army, he concedes, but "if we are ever accused of that we will show that we have no clear-cut chain of command, no uniforms

and no pay." No army, in other words, and a minimum of coordination, although DePugh says most of the members
would prefer closer coordination. He adds, "We're only ex-
ercising our constitutional rights of freedom to bear arms,
freedom of assembly and freedom of speech."

Another Minutemen undertaking is to broaden the base of
the organization by offering training in self-protection "to all
loyal Americans." A series of "semi-open" schools was
planned for this purpose. The first was held in St. Louis in
1962. Notice was passed by word of mouth and, when newspapers would take them, by classified ads. Since Minutemen
as well as others are in attendance, DePugh says, the advantage of publicly advertised schools is obvious: if authorities or Communists investigate the seminar they will not
be able to tell who is a Minuteman and who is not; therefore,
they will not be able to keep a blacklist for future use against
the Minutemen.

Placing classified ads is also a favored means of general
recruiting; it is a continuing project. "Join the Minutemen,"
a typical ad reads, "an organization of loyal Americans dedicated to the preservation of both national and individual
freedom. Help put real strength into civilian defense. Pledge
yourself and your rifle to a free America. For full details write
Minutemen, 613 East Alton, Independence."

This is only a mailing address. A sign-painter rents the
building there from DePugh; he says Minutemen mail is re-
directed by the post office and he never sees it. DePugh
says the organization's headquarters, containing its printing
equipment and some supplies, is elsewhere in Independence.
He refuses to say where. Other Minutemen consider headquarters to be Norborne, now the home of DePugh's
$400,000-a-year pharmaceutical business, which is housed in
a long, low, warehouselike plant on the main street. DePugh's
neighbors refer to it as "the pill factory," but despite the in-
timacy of life in a small rural village do not venture through

the Biolab Corporation plant and have not, in most cases, become acquainted with the owner. He stays to himself, they say.

DePugh says the Birch Society, of which he is a member, has some "intelligent and sincere" people who have "given a lot of thought to the problem of Communism." But he considers the approach of most Rightist organizations ineffective.

"These people think they can talk their way to victory," he says. "I don't think we can. My group is more or less resigned to a Communist takeover of the United States, either from within or without."

So he continues to hold "guerrilla warfare" seminars throughout the country.

Minutemen bands study scouting, infiltration of positions, and hand-to-hand combat. They tinker with all manner of weaponry that could be handled by small groups, from pistols to antitank guns. They also familiarize themselves with Russian weapons in case they ever have to use them. DePugh says they can be purchased from several sources.

DePugh counsels each defender of the country to study every foot of ground of his local area "so if we have to shoot it out with the Communists we'll have the terrain advantage over them." He says he has gone over his part of Missouri so he won't have to rely on guesswork.

"We study the tactics of guerrilla warfare the way some people study chess," he explains, "as an intellectual pursuit."

Much of the training is done at night, he says, "because that's when an underground can operate." Part of the challenge is to cover tracks so well the maneuvers go undetected. Minutemen are advised at their seminars not to fight pitched battles with regular troops and to stay friendly with the civilian population.

DePugh says the Minutemen have units in Canada and are in touch with similar groups in Europe.

Despite the inherent dangers to society from Minutemen

activities and aims, authorities have been inclined to relegate these country commandos to the nutty fringe as essentially harmless. Their preference for the woodsy over the political reinforces this view. So do their inflated membership claims, including their original goal of a million adherents by 1963. Their list of suspects can be taken no more seriously than Welch's list of liberals. The use to which they put their patriotic impulses properly subjects them to Hargis' assessment of "boys playing soldier." Still, the fascistic implications of their para-military approach to combating communism is embarrassing even to such extremists as Robert Welch. He dismisses the Minutemen organization (occasionally and facetiously called the armed division of the Birch Society because of the overlapping membership) as "a foolish idea."

10:
Assorted

The cover of the 36-page booklet reads:

FIRST NATIONAL DIRECTORY
of "Rightist" Groups, Publications and Some
Individuals in the United States
Fourth Edition
Price: $2.00

Even this ambitious undertaking (by the Alert Americans
Association, Post Office Box 1222, Los Angeles 53) falls short
by far of listing all Right-wing organizations. Although it includes more than 1800, with addresses from California to
New York and Florida to Horse Cave, Kentucky, a Washington investigator says that as many as a dozen organizations
of the Ultra Right are formed each week. Few become nationally known and many appear and disappear at the whisk
of a printed letterhead.

Not all the organizations in the directory belong to the Radical Right. The American Legion is listed along with the John
Birch Society and the Minutemen. Segregationist groups and
anti-Semitic associations are included as well as organiza-

126

tions lobbying against foreign aid. A study by the Anti-Defamation League of the B'nai B'rith considered only 282 of the groups, 121 of them formed in 1961, to be in the Radical Right, or militantly anticommunist, category. The 282 did not include organizations that were considered basically anti-Semitic or anti-Negro. The leadership of the Birch, Schwarz, and some other groups resent being lumped with organizations with anti-Jewish or anti-Negro bias.

From 1957 to 1961 the number of American vigilantes grew rapidly. The "third edition" of the "Rightist directory," in 1960, had listed just a few more than a thousand groups, compared with the 1800 of 1961.

Some of these groups, including those that consist just of a "patriot," his wife, a mimeograph machine, and a mailing list, have been in business for years. For all of them, a program, a newsletter, and a "line" are basic equipment. A few have shifted from crude allegations to a more sophisticated approach. Some now have respectable-looking offices that turn out professionally printed newsletters and pamphlets. But flashy or ragged, the message is similar. Few appeal to the intellect; most tap emotion. Some organizations are local, such as the Pasadena Committee for Exposing Subversive Activities, Inc. Others, such as We, The People!, are national. Memberships frequently overlap. Even boards of directors and trustees often contain many of the same names.

We, The People! (the exclamation point is part of the name) has headquarters in a three-room office suite in downtown Chicago. For fifty cents a month it offers panaceas for a number of political problems. Its president is white-haired, soft-spoken Harry T. Everingham, who says the organization has members in 1700 communities in fifty states. Who are they? Well, the names are "confidential." "Our enemy," he says, "doesn't disclose its figures."

We, The People! had its beginnings in fundamentalist evangelism, as did some other organizations of the Far Right.

In 1952, the Rev. James Fifield founded the Freedom Club of Downtown Chicago. Fifield moved to Los Angeles, where, as pastor of one of California's largest churches, the independent First Congregational Church, he set up Freedom Clubs similar in their programs to We, The People! and started a Right-wing radio series called "The Lighted Window." The group he left behind in Chicago became We, The People! in 1955.

The principal effort of We, The People! is propaganda for the repeal of the federal income tax. For fifty cents a month members get a bulletin called "Free Enterprise," which plumps for a "liberty amendment" to the United States Constitution. This is the Birch-supported "Twenty-fourth Amendment" intended to force the government to sell to private industry the businesses it owns or operates and to repeal the graduated income tax. "Unless we awaken the American people," Everingham says, "we're going to have socialism, and socialism is communism." Elected national chairman of the organization in 1962 was Ezra Taft Benson, Secretary of Agriculture for eight years under Eisenhower. (At about the same time, Benson's son Reed was appointed Utah coordinator of the John Birch Society. His father, applauding the step, called the Society the most effective nonchurch organization "in our fight against creeping socialism and godless communism.")

We, The People! labors mainly on the political front. It wants its members to organize in their communities to defeat "socialist" candidates for public office. It has had little success so far, evidently because it is difficult to make the income tax appear a nonessential frill.

To get the liberty amendment passed is the sole purpose of another national organization, the Committee for Economic Freedom, with headquarters in Los Angeles. Resolutions calling for the repeal of the income tax have been adopted in Wyoming, Georgia, Texas, Nevada, South Carolina, and

Louisiana. In other states the issue is revived frequently. In North Dakota, for instance, the lower house passed such a resolution in 1961. It was defeated in the state senate after a bitter fight. The movement seeks resolutions in 34 states, the two-thirds necessary to force Congress to act.

Also at war with the income tax is Brigadier General Bonner Fellers, retired, in business at 1001 Connecticut Avenue in Washington, D.C. Fellers, an aide to General Douglas MacArthur during World War II, is national director of a political-action group called For America and chairman of the Citizens' Foreign Aid Committee. He says For America has five major objectives—elimination of the income tax, termination of the peacetime draft, maintenance of superior air power, withdrawal of the U.S. from the UN, and removal of the UN from the U.S. Fellers also favors an end to "compulsory unionism" and seeks full-scale congressional investigations into "Communist-socialist" activities.

Wearing his Citizens' Foreign Aid Committee hat, the general told a congressional committee that the government must bring American troops home from Germany and halt aid to NATO countries. The United States, says General Fellers, must prepare to stand alone and count on air power as its major defense.

Board members of the Citizens' Foreign Aid Committee include retired Generals Albert C. Wedemeyer and George E. Stratemeyer, J. Bracken Lee, also a board member of We, The People! and Clarence Manion, publisher and broadcaster of the Manion Forum and a member of the Birch Council.

Some businessmen are finding the philosophy of the Far Right useful fare for increasing business. Richfield Oil, which sponsored Fred Schwarz' big rally at the Hollywood Bowl, reported little objection from its customers. One executive remarked that customers were coming in to fill up their tanks with "some of that anti-Commie gas."

One of the innovators of anticommunism for commerce is

one of the nation's largest savings and loan companies, Coast
Federal of Los Angeles. Its "free-enterprise department"
sends millions of tracts, pamphlets, and flyers to depositors,
borrowers, and business concerns—at a cost to Coast Federal
of up to 4 per cent of its net income before taxes. One of
Coast Federal's projects was to reprint (from the *Congressional Record*) and distribute thousands of copies of a defense of the John Birch Society by former Representative
Rousselot.

Shirley Black, the young executive in charge of the "department of free enterprise," believes that about 2000 other
American businesses have similar operations. Joe Crail, Coast
Federal's president, says: "Anticommunism builds sales and
raises employee performance."

Crail and his company hew to the Hard Right line. One
pamphlet distributed by the free-enterprise department proclaims: "Since we are at war, cultural exchanges amount to
nothing more than weapons of espionage, propaganda, and
sources of income for the Communist conspiracy." Another
takes the Birch line: "America is declining as the 'majority
mob' reaches for divine rights to rule over the individual."

One provocative card, distributed in batches of thousands,
quoted Premier Khrushchev of the Soviet Union as saying:
"We cannot expect the Americans to jump from Capitalism
to Communism, but we can assist their elected leaders in
giving Americans small doses of Socialism, until they suddenly awake to find they have Communism." This has been
widely used in Far Right propaganda as documentary evidence of the conspiracy and danger from within the United
States. Senator Lee Metcalf, Montana Democrat, asked the
Library of Congress, the FBI, the United States Information
Agency, the State Department, and the Central Intelligence
Agency about it. None could find a record of Khrushchev
having made the statement. John McCone, C.I.A. director,
wrote Metcalf: "We believe the quotation to be spurious."

Metcalf said in a Senate speech that such material leads Americans to believe "that their President, their senators, their representatives, their judges and their local officials are Communist stooges. Thus a lie is used to perpetrate a greater lie. Whoever created this quotation, and those who, knowing it to be spurious, nevertheless disseminate it, are cut from the same cloth as Communists and Fascists."

The card was withdrawn after it could not be substantiated, but by then Coast Federal and Poor Richard's Book Shop, a Right-wing outlet in Hollywood, had printed nearly a million copies.

Coast Federal's free-enterprise department also has provided booklets and speakers for many of Los Angeles County's 1500 public schools. It offers a manual for speakers and teachers, and distributes thousands of copies of it. It distributes posters to high schools and colleges and makes cash awards for Americanism essays. It sponsors speakers and film showings for school, civic, service, church, and political groups.

In 1962 the Los Angeles County Federation of Labor challenged the program, saying: "Coast Federal management's wild charges, anti-democratic bias, blind attacks on programs of social progress and indiscriminate use of the label 'Communist' do not inspire confidence in its ability to make sound judgments on the subject of communism."

Coast Federal has continued to spend about a quarter of a million dollars a year on the program.

"It's good business," Crail says.

California holds no patent on the idea. A furniture dealer in Georgia is one of hundreds of small storekeepers who distribute Schwarz anti-Communism comic books with the company's name printed on the back. A Milwaukee automatic controls manufacturer prints thousands of copies of the doctor's congressional testimony and buys radio time for Right-wing commentators. Other companies set up seminars in their plants on either a voluntary or "must attend" basis and then send "trained" executives into the community to proselytize.

In the Chicago suburb of Bensenville, one of the best-organized company programs has been working quietly and —its leaders say—effectively. In 1961 Frank Flick, president of the Flick-Reedy Corp., formed the tax-exempt Flick-Reedy Education Association and began holding anti-Communist seminars in the company auditorium. Since then, the company, the nation's largest manufacturer of pneumatic cylinders for piston machines, has enlarged its activities. The association has six men who lecture and organize throughout Illinois and prepare packaged tape-recorded and slide seminars for local groups. Far Right professionals are brought in to lecture. They frequently use material put out by the National Education Program at Harding College.

Employees at Flick-Reedy attend the seminars and see the films on company time, just as they may also take non-political courses in letter writing and driver training at company expense. Flick also pays the tuition for employees to take courses at Chicago's Institute for Economic Inquiry. The Institute is supported by companies that send "group leaders" to study prior to conducting seminars in their own plants or offices. The director of the school, John Monroe, believes there is no need for government aid programs or for governmental restrictions on business.

Operating on a much larger scale and in a different way is Texas oilman H. L. Hunt, who believes business advertising and patriotism go together. He combines them in a newsletter and radio broadcasts, both called Life Lines. It is estimated that Hunt reaches several million people every day.

The radio series is conducted by the Rev. Wayne Poucher and is heard on more than 200 radio stations. A television version also has been produced. Often Hunt's HLH canned goods are advertised at intervals throughout Poucher's lectures.

The lectures start with a quiet and deliberate recital of the threat of atheistic communism from overseas and end with Poucher striking hard at subversion from within: "The other threat is from the inside, a slower, more subtle force, but, in the end, almost as deadly as communism. Big government is rapidly betraying us into socialism through the medium of the welfare state. . . . First came the income tax, now graduated to the point of confiscation in the higher brackets. An ever-growing clamor for welfare and security has played into the hands of the planners who offer many programs in the name of humanity and security." These planners, according to Poucher, are socialists who "today chart much of the course of our lives and . . . are continually grasping for new areas of control."

Basically, that is the "Hunt line," offered in the mellifluous tones of a rural Southern Church of Christ pastor who is heard today by more people (by Life Lines estimate) than the 25,000,000 who listened to the Amos and Andy program at the highest point of its popularity.

Hunt's Life Line newsletter is published three times a week from Washington, where Life Line Foundation, established in 1958, shares a building with the Far Right weekly *Human Events*. Readers are urged to subscribe and to join Life Line Links, a "freedom crusade." Links mails out copies of Poucher's radio lectures and conducts essay contests against the United Nations, foreign aid, and taxes. Life Lines operates as a nonprofit, nondenominational, patriotic and religious corporation and is tax-exempt.

When a new extremist movement arises, there frequently are rumors that Hunt is supporting it. He says these reports are overstated. Hunt estimates his expenditure in behalf of furthering his own views to be less than a million dollars a

year. An archconservative, he prefers to be called "construc-
tive." He says that Communists, fellow travelers, and Fascists
are "the mistaken enemies of freedom"—"the Mistaken" for
short. Hunt says he will not impugn the motives of liberals
because many liberals "are as dedicated to America as I am."
He adds that the dangerous people are middle-of-the-roaders
who will not stand up "for right or wrong."

In Los Angeles, D. B. Lewis is another businessman
who presses and pays for the Far Right cause. He believes
that merchandising the philosophy of the ultras is good for
the Lewis Food Company, which sells dog food and other
pet products. He is also president of the Organization to
Repeal Federal Income Taxes, Inc.

Lewis doesn't temper his political pronouncements. "The
income tax is one of the most vicious laws ever passed," he
says. He warns that "Communists are invading our churches,
schools, colleges and communications." His answer to American problems is simple: "I'd blast the Communists off the
map in twenty-four hours."

Lewis is a sponsor of the "Dan Smoot Report" on thirty-two
television and fifty-two radio stations in eleven western states.
Dan Smoot readily admits being guilty of what his opponents
call "extremism." The well-spoken former FBI agent from
Texas says, "I equate the growth of the welfare state with
socialism and socialism with Communism." He says three
major television networks turned down his request for time
but that he was able to muster heavy economic pressure to
get on the air. Both on and off, Smoot makes his charges in
a well-enunciated, authoritative manner that holds a listener
whether he agrees or not. His is probably the most successful
"single" act on the Far Right. Local chapters of the John
Birch Society have made projects of finding sponsorship for
him in their areas, even though he says he is not a member.

"I wondered," Smoot says, "when I was a member of the
FBI's Commie squad, why those who opposed communism

were vilified and slandered. I learned the reason. It was because people were blindly following the philosophy of the New Deal, which stands for the total transfer of power from the individual to the Federal Government under the claim of using the power beneficently. This is the same philosophy of the Fair Deal, the New Frontier, and modern Republicanism. It is also the basic philosophy of communism, fascism and nazism."

In 1941, with bachelor's and master's degrees from Southern Methodist University, Smoot went to Harvard as a teaching fellow in English. He joined the Federal Bureau of Investigation before finishing work for a doctorate.

Smoot quit the FBI after nine and a half years to work for Hunt as moderator of Facts Forum, Life Lines' predecessor, on radio in the early 1950s. In 1955 he branched out on his own. Besides his radio and television work, he publishes a weekly newsletter, which is also called the *Dan Smoot Report.*

The American Security Council is another enterprise run by a former FBI agent, John M. Fisher. The Council spends a quarter of a million dollars a year culling information and providing reports to more than 3400 member companies on programs, individuals or organizations that members have asked about preparatory to providing speakers, financial support, endorsement, or employment. Fisher, the president, says the files, at the Chicago headquarters and a West Coast office in Los Angeles, constitute the largest private library on Communist activities in the country.

The files come from a variety of sources, including material bought from the estate of the late Harry Jung, who ran the old American Vigilante Intelligence Federation in Chicago, from back issues of the *Worker,* and from the more than 6000 publications that are clipped each week.

The Council, formed in 1955 to "keep a continuing check on the Communist threat," publishes a Newsletter and Washington Report which purport to offer inside intelligence information on matters of national security. Editor of the Washington Report is Frank J. Johnson, author of *No Substitute for Victory,* which calls for taking Albania and other "real estate" away from the Communists to show Premier Khrushchev "that we intend to create plenty of trouble for him in his own back yard."

Fisher says the Council limits its published reports to security matters, takes no stand on "political" questions, and cannot be classified as "Right Wing" or anything else in the political realm.

Helping in the formulation of policy is the Council's national strategy committee, of which General Wedemeyer and Admiral Ben Moreell, retired, are members.

Moreell also is chairman of the board—and General Fellers is vice-chairman—of a political-action group called Americans for Constitutional Action. Started by *Human Events,* it publishes a detailed index of the voting records of congressmen, rating each as to his conservatism. In 1961, for example, Senator Paul Douglas, Illinois Democrat, was scored as voting "right" on 11 per cent of the issues tabulated, while his fellow Illinois senator, Republican Everett McKinley Dirksen, scored 77. (The Courtneys' voting index, with fewer issues on the scorecard, gave Douglas 0 and Dirksen 64 that year.) For the Eighty-seventh Congress (1961–62), Senator Tower scored 100 while his Texas colleague, Democrat Ralph W. Yarborough, got only 4. Goldwater received 100 compared with 12 for the other Arizonan, Democrat Carl Hayden. Senator Thurmond's 100 contrasted with 32 for his South Carolina colleague, Olin D. Johnston. Sixteen with perfect scores in the House included Representatives Hiestand, Rousselot, Scherer, and Alger. Many conservatives regard the indices as yardsticks of a congressman's worth, just as many liberals read the ratings compiled by Americans for Democratic Action and the Committee on Political Education of the AFL–CIO.

In the 1962 election campaign, Americans for Constitutional Action assigned field men to aid forty-six conservative candidates for Congress. Their identity was kept secret, Moreell said, because publicity "might jeopardize the candidate." He said the object was to elect men pledged to "safeguard the God-given dignity of the individual and fight against appeasement of the Communists and a socialized economy through centralization of power in a mammoth bureaucratic government." The purpose of the ACA is to elect conservatives in order to "reverse the current massive movement of our Nation into Socialism and a regimented society."

A Far Right organization of national import is the Cardinal Mindszenty Foundation, with more than 3000 study groups in forty-nine states. It claims it has the largest Roman Catholic following on the Far Right except for the John Birch Society, which Welch has said is 40 per cent Catholic. The Foundation was formed in St. Louis in 1958 and is directed by a council that includes three archbishops in exile who were forced out of their dioceses in China and North Korea. Eleanor Schlafly, executive secretary, says the foundation seeks no political action, merely furnishes "educational material on atheistic communism" from a small St. Louis office. A sample press release lists, without documentation, these Communist goals:

> Intensified efforts to capture American youth by propaganda magazines, student and teacher exchanges with Communist countries, widespread distribution of pornographic material at the high school and college level, increase in morally-offensive movies and paperback books, promotion of pro-Communist lecturers on college compuses . . . and the mobilization of college students into Red fronts and student "peace" organizations. . . .

Admission of Red China into the United Nations through persuasion of U.S. and UN officials that it is "inevitable." . . .

Paralysis of the House Un-American Activities Committee and Senate Internal Security Subcommittee through student protests, defiant witnesses, harangues about civil rights and cuts in appropriations.

A summit conference.

Conquest of Quemoy and Matsu by selling Americans the false slogans that they are "militarily indefensible" and that to defend them would "start World War Three."

Use of student riots . . . to force removal of Chiang Kai-shek and other anti-Communist stalwarts.

Capture of West Berlin and Formosa under the ruse of turning them over to a UN trusteeship.

Promotion of the Red lie that a "break" between Soviet Russia and Red China is imminent.

Theft of the Panama Canal from the U.S. under the guise of "internationalization" by the UN or "nationalization" by Panama.

Accelerated campaign to overthrow or "neutralize" Latin American governments [with] . . . a cadre of Red students trained in political warfare schools in Moscow and Prague.

Pincer propaganda campaign to end American cooperation with leading Catholic statesmen Adenauer, De Gaulle, Franco and Salazar; and to continue American aid to bitter anti-Catholics such as Tito.

. . . offer special inducements to promote American trade with the Soviet Union, Red China and other Communist countries and greatly expand cultural exchanges in all fields.

Infiltration and smearing of anti-Communist groups by paid crackpots and hired disseminators of "hate" literature.

Stephen Dunker, a Vincentian priest who founded the organization, named it after Cardinal Mindszenty because of the Catholic and anti-Communist connotation of the name.

Other foundations on the Far Right include the Veritas Foundation, alarmed chiefly by the teaching of Keynesian economists. The Foundation's stated purpose is "to educate the staffs, students and alumni of American colleges and universities on communism."

Another, the Freedom Foundation, gives patriotic awards, organizes educational programs, and points out "un-American" thinking. Its president, Kenneth Wells, while lecturing at a Project Alert seminar on the West Coast, suddenly shouted toward the TV cameras:

"I want to talk to you Marxists and traitors out there. I know you're glued to your TV screens. Get this and get it straight. Get the message! Comrades, this country's twenty-year sleep is over!"

At the same session, Colonel Mitchell Paige, a retired Marine Corps Medal of Honor winner, quietly told a morning session that he believed Chief Justice Warren should be hanged. Later he apologized, wryly reporting that the desire to hang the Chief Justice just "comes over me" sometimes.

Freedom-in-Action, a Houston-based semi-secret society, employs vigilante methods in a search for "Communist sympathizers." The organization, formed in 1960, is endorsed by Welch as one Birchers should support. Its members swear not to be "captured and taken over by subversives." Its guidebook states, among other things, that members are to "stamp out the poison of communism whether labeled as liberalism, socialism, welfare statism or communism." Members work for "patriotic" candidates for political office.

A group called the Minutewomen searches for Communists in PTAs, school libraries, and elsewhere on the local level. Chapters in several cities are chartered from a national headquarters in Los Angeles.

The Daughters of the American Revolution received some more of its periodic publicity for ultraconservatism at its 1962 convention when Major Arch Roberts, who had administered Edwin Walker's militant anti-Communist program in Germany, charged before the women's organization that several government officials had "leftist leanings." The Army dismissed him. The DAR protested, demanding that Congress investigate this "arbitrary exercise of power."

Another militarist on the Far Right is retired Brigadier General Herbert C. Holdridge, who established the Constitutional Provisional Government of the United States in Sherman Oaks, California. General Holdridge, who also has his own Minuteman unit, produces bulletins that have called American Catholics "traitors," American elections "rigged," and newspaper, radio, and television companies "treasonous."

In Cincinnati, M. G. Lowman's Circuit Riders, Inc., publishes handbooks and bulletins "documenting" subversion in the churches. In one he purports to show that thirty of the ninety-five persons who prepared the Revised Standard Version of the Bible were "Communist fellow travelers." Lowman's pamphlets and compendiums often are for sale at Rightist meetings.

Another list-maker is Verne Kaub of Madison, Wisconsin, who heads the American Council of Christian Laymen. Kaub's pamphlet "How Red Is The National Council of Churches?" charges that a large number of clergymen affiliated with the National Council are Communists.

There are at least a score of fundamentalist churchmen who have joined the professional anticommunist trade. Aside from Hargis, none has been more successful than Carl McIntire, who was instrumental in bringing Fred Schwarz to the United States. After McIntire was dropped from the Presbyterian ministry in 1936 for "disapproval, defiance and acts in contravention" of church law, he went to work on his own. The Bible Presbyterian church he formed grew to about

5500 members. From this home church, McIntire formed the American Council of Christian Churches and an international counterpart. Both groups make open war on the National Council and World Council of Churches. The American Council claims the allegiance of fourteen small fundamentalist denominations with congregations totaling more than 3,000,000. From his headquarters at Collingswood, New Jersey, McIntire publishes the *Christian Beacon* and records a daily radiocast that offers the message of the Far Right.

McIntire's ally and protégé, Edgar Bundy of Wheaton, Illinois, operates the Church League of America. He, too, says the National Council of Churches has Communist sympathizers. Bundy, who was an Air Force major in intelligence in World War II, formed the Abraham Lincoln Republican Club to recapture the GOP, he says, from New Dealers and Internationalists. In the 1950s, as chairman of an American Legion antisubversive committee, he championed McCarthy and gained national attention when he attacked the Girl Scouts as Communist-oriented. Bundy holds "countersubversive" seminars that favor getting the U.S. out of the UN, formation of study committees to find Red influence in textbooks, and establishment of a loyalty oath for state employees.

At the bottom of any scale of curiosities of the Far Right is George Lincoln Rockwell's American Nazi Party. It is discounted even by most inhabitants of the Right, but Rockwell continues to claim them as ideological companions. Edwin Walker, Rockwell says, would make a good leader for a national coalition of patriots.

Rockwell and his brown-shirted followers first called attention to themselves from a three-story headquarters house in Arlington, Virginia, where a sagging tin roof covers the yellow frame building and a sign over the door proclaims: "American Nazi Party Headquarters. Trespassers will be prosecuted or shot."

Rockwell, a former Navy commander, says he has about fifty members in Virginia and "fine organizations in Chicago, Los Angeles, New York, New Orleans, Boston and quite a few other places."

In Virginia the state legislature has forbidden him to use the name "Nazi" and has revoked his incorporation papers. In Chicago, his "fine organization" is limited to a very small group of men and youths. When Rockwell and some of his followers showed up in New Orleans, in what was called a "Hate Bus," they were run out of town and, upon their return, arrested.

"When we take power," says Rockwell, "we'll appropriate fifty billion dollars to build a modern industrial nation in Africa and offer ten thousand dollars to every nigger family to migrate there. No one would be forced to return but niggers who stayed here would be rigidly segregated—on reservations."

Jews? Eighty per cent, says Rockwell, are traitors. He would kill them.

Another Nazilike group, the American Renaissance Party, is older brother to Rockwell's organization. At Schwarz' appearance in New York's Manhattan Center, Renaissance pickets marched outside the hall and distributed handbills demanding that Jews be exposed as subverting the militant anti-Communist movement. The words were obviously aimed at Schwarz, whose father was a Jew in Austria before he became a convert to Christianity and emigrated to Australia.

The Renaissance Party is run by a longtime professional anti-Semite, James Madole. The mimeographed flyer handed out the night of the Schwarz rally proclaimed:

"The National Renaissance Party wishes to expose the nefarious methods used by this phony 'kosher conservative' leadership to divert the efforts and activities of true patriots into the wrong channels! .... Are you aware that every effort is being made by Jewish conservatives like Barry Goldwater,

Roy Cohn, Dr. Fred Schwarz . . . to discredit and undermine such gentile patriots as Major General Edwin Walker and Robert Welch?"

Among other organizations that qualify for the lunatic fringe of the Far Right is the "National States' Rights Party" with headquarters at Jeffersonville, Indiana. Its brochure is decorated with a thunderbolt and the slogan is "White Men Unite." Dozens of such groups exist in the Deep South, in the Midwest, and in California.

The Realpolitical Institute calls for the "immediate discharge of all alien non-Whites, members of the disloyal Jewish Consensus, Internationalists, Pacifists, Communists, and Liberals from all local, State, and Federal governments and armed forces."

Then there is the American Coalition of Patriotic Societies, which calls itself "an organization to co-ordinate the efforts of Patriotic, Civic and Fraternal Societies To Keep America American." Operating on a similar theme is a group called the American Action Council. In Pasadena is the Network of Patriotic Letter Writers, in Columbus, Ohio, the Watch Washington Club.

The list is long. Tomorrow it will have new names. It will, that is, if the Far Right continues to manifest itself in the disarray of proliferating groups that has been the pattern in recent years.

three:
The Fray

11:

In Print

SHOW YOUR COLORS, urged the banner in the window of the new *American Opinion* Library of Fort Wayne, Indiana. The "flag holidays" were listed and a prominently displayed American flag caught the eyes of shoppers on the busy downtown street early in 1963. FLAGS, CONSERVATIVE LITERATURE, RENTAL LIBRARY, said a sign. JOHN BIRCH MATERIAL AVAILABLE HERE, proclaimed another. Books in the window included *Decline of the American Republic* by John T. Flynn; *Communist America—Must It Be?* by Billy James Hargis, and *The Key to Peace* by Clarence Manion. Hundreds more were neatly arranged for browsing inside.

Bookstores and libraries of the Movement have sprung up all over the country, their shelves stocked with printed and tape-recorded propaganda. The Birch Society opened *American Opinion* libraries in various cities and suburbs with selected literature for sale or rent. The first Far Right bookstores were in the Los Angeles area. Poor Richard's opened in 1960; the next year the Betsy Ross Bookshop, the Minute-

man, the Heritage Book Shoppe, and the Freedom Bookstore
were in business nearby. Soon others, from the Pro-Blue
Patriotic Book Store in the Los Angeles cluster to the Joe
McCarthy Book Store in South Boston, had opened from
coast to coast.

The bookshops also serve as meeting places of Far Right
activists. Pictures of the heroes of the Right—Welch, Walker,
McCarthy, Schwarz, Hargis, and others—decorate the walls.
The stores often have a red, white, and blue color scheme.
There is usually a rack or table where tape-recorded exhorta-
tions by leaders of the Movement are offered. The stores also
sell "This is a Republic" stickers, "Impeach Warren" bumper
strips, and other novelties.

But these stores are small operations. The bulk of the Far
Right's business goes to several mail-order distributors. The
Bookmailer, in New York, offers the greatest selection and
does the biggest business. Its largest volume is in publications of the soft-cover or tract variety. Run by Lyle Munson,
a former Central Intelligence Agency agent, the company
in 1961 sold more than two million pieces of printed matter.

Among the authors who have a following on the Far Right
are Robert Strausz-Hupé of the University of Pennsylvania,
Russell Kirk, and novelist Ayn Rand. Goldwater books sell
well. On another plane is the work of such writers as Hargis
and Schwarz. Their books—and especially their inexpensive
tracts and pamphlets—are the best sellers.

Another favorite is W. Cleon Skousen's *The Naked Communist*. After sixteen years with the FBI, five years on the
faculty of Brigham Young University, four as Salt Lake City's
police chief, and a term as field director of the American Security Council, Skousen has divided his time between writing, lecturing, and directing the *Freedom University of the
Air*, a series of sixty-five half-hour television programs for
use by local stations with local sponsorship. His book, the
jacket says, supplies "in one exciting, readable volume the

whole incredible story of communism ... graphically told."

The Naked Communist offers a mixture of history, politics, and religion to support the author's contention that "no man who knows what lies behind the lethal Communist program of 'co-existence' would dare accept that proposal as a long range solution."

In 1962 the Courtneys contributed another volume to the library of the Far Right, a book called *America's Unelected Rulers,* which purports to describe a plan to "destroy America's national sovereignty, subvert the U.S. Constitution via NATO and the Atlantic Community, and put the United States under control of a Socialist-dominated world government."

The Courtneys say the book outlines "the plans of the Council on Foreign Relations to ultimately by-pass the U.S. Congress and set up a Socialist One-World Government staffed by 'private citizens,' the U.S. membership of which would, of course, be under the direction of the Council on Foreign Relations."

Billy James Hargis then added another "exposé," *The Facts About Communism and Our Churches,* citing as sources for his findings of skulduggery in the clergy such authorities as Lowman, Philbrick, and numerous former Communists and counterspies for the FBI.

Another favorite among Far Right readers is Rosalie M. Gordon's *Nine Men Against America,* a diatribe against the Supreme Court. Her book is gospel to those in the impeach-Warren ranks; it is endorsed by the John Birch Society and sold through Welch's organization. The book asks how the reader would like to have a Communist teaching in his schools or representing him in court. Miss Gordon says such questions must be answered now because of the effect recent Supreme Court decisions could have. She adds: "In the light of this whole sorry record of the court's usurpation of the rights of states and citizens, and the terrifying go-ahead signal it has given to the Communist conspiracy in America, we need not be surprised at the jubilation in communist circles over the Supreme Court of the United States." In her summary she requests that "you and other Americans demand that Congress rescue from the nine usurpers on the bench the tattered charter of freedom, repair it, and restore it to the people."

Miss Gordon is on the staff of America's Future, which examines textbooks to ascertain whether they are fit for use in American schoolrooms.

Toward Soviet America is another of the most popular books on the Ultras' shelf. It is praised in an introduction by Representative Francis Walter, chairman of the House Committee on Un-American Activities, as "the book the Communists tried to destroy." *Toward Soviet America* was written in 1932 by William Z. Foster, longtime chairman of the American Communist Party. According to Walter, *Toward Soviet America* disclosed "exactly what those geniuses of evil [Marx, Lenin, and Stalin] planned for this country under the hammer and sickle. The plan has not changed. *Toward Soviet America* still reveals what your fate under that symbol of slavery is intended to be."

Most of the Far Right books bear imprints of publishers that are little known generally. *Toward Soviet America* is labeled as a "product of Elgin Enterprises, Inc." The publisher's address is a post-office box number on Balboa Island, California. Skousen's book was put out by the Ensign Publishing Company, Salt Lake City. Miss Gordon's was published by Devin-Adair of New York, which—like Henry Regnery of Chicago—issues among other titles a large number of Rightist works.

Except for sale at the specialized bookshops, at "seminars," or through the mails, these volumes are seldom seen. They are advertised in *National Review, American Mercury,* and in the newsletters and monthly memos of Far Right organizations. Some of the larger distributors, such as Bookmailer and the Freedom Bookshelf of Lombard, Illinois, send out catalogues listing books "especially selected to help start your study of liberty." They also offer a variety of reprints of reports issued by the Senate Internal Security Sub-committee and the House Committee on Un-American Activities.

A typical Bookmailer ad in *American Opinion* offered *No Wonder We Are Losing,* by Robert Morris; McCarthy's *America's Retreat from Victory;* Bundy's *Collectivism in the Churches;* and Welch's *The Life of John Birch,* along with a dozen others.

Weekly and monthly magazines and bulletins are the Far Right's most important media of indoctrination. A leading disseminator of the Far Right's point of view is the Washingington newsletter *Human Events.* Its 1962 circulation was 107,000. The eighteen-year-old weekly had only 13,000 subscribers in 1960, and before that had struggled along on the verge of collapse. With the upsurge of Right-wing activity it grew to a million-dollar-a-year business. One issue offered a spirited defense of restrictive immigration laws by Congressman Walter. Another, widely reprinted, offered Edwin Walker a forum for charges that the military was being muzzled. Another, all cartoons, pointed out that there was no difference between the "iron chains of Communism" and the "silken cords of Socialism" in making the individual the slave of government.

Of growing appeal to conservative intellectuals has been William Buckley's *National Review,* biweekly with a 1962 circulation of 72,000. In the same issue in which Buckley denounced Welch there was an attack on Christianity's social gospel, a full-page ad for a "world freedom rally" by the Young Americans for Freedom, and a classified ad for the McGuffey's Readers of the last century, reissued to satisfy conservatives' demands for grade-school texts that stressed patriotism and self-reliance.

Further to the Right is the *Dan Smoot Report*. This well-printed ten-page weekly newsletter doubled its circulation to 40,000 copies in 1961.

Smoot's line seldom varies. Volume 7, No. 28 (Broadcast 320) of September 18, 1961, is typical. In it he charged that all attempts to discredit his kind of Americanism were dictated by the Kremlin to its "tools" in the United States. "In the United States," Smoot wrote, "the government itself, many of the biggest churches and church organizations (like the National Council of Churches), most of the big tax-exempt foundations, many of the colleges and universities and a powerful array of tax-exempt organizations (which I have previously characterized as constituting the invisible government of the United States)—all relentlessly bombard the American population with internationalist world-mindedness propaganda which communist leaders urge as the primary way to soften up a nation."

The *Dan Smoot Report* sells for $10 a year and includes a picture of the handsome oracle at the top of page 1 of every issue.

Clarence E. Manion of South Bend, Indiana, also puts his picture on his publication, *The Manion Forum*, an attractive weekly newsletter that consists of transcripts of a radio and television program of the same name. The program is carried on more than 200 stations, many of them in Western states—where Lewis, the dog-food man, is a sponsor.

Manion, former dean of Notre Dame's Law School, conducts the operation from his law office in the northern Indiana city. Each week he offers the microphone to an "expert on communism" or some other patriotic American who proceeds to tell Manion and the audience how the United States is being threatened by communism.

Manion fights the income tax, defends Walker, and describes himself as an unreconstructed McCarthyite. He sells the newsletter and solicits contributions. Corporate support is reported to be more than half a million dollars a year.

Manion is an original member of the National Council of the John Birch Society. A colleague on the Council, Father Richard Ginder, is a featured columnist of *Our Sunday Visitor*, a national Roman Catholic week-end paper read in more than 960,000 homes. This writer translates Welch into written Sunday sermons with conviction and cleverness.

Father Ginder is preoccupied with the Red conspiracy. In one column he made these observations:

"Somewhere here or abroad there is an individual, Mr. X, coordinating intelligence and strategy for the Enemy conquest of this country. He is very likely an American with his desk in Washington or New York.

"Now, for an example of conspiracy at work: Comes news through various leaks that the United States is mounting an invasion of Cuba. It must be stopped. Every possible means is used without success. In desperation at the last minute, Mr. X says, 'Our man Schwarz is a close friend of Weiss, who happens to have a high place in the American delegation to the United Nations. Schwarz must somehow convince Weiss that if the Air Force is used it will turn all of Latin America against the United States.'

"Thus, wheels move within wheels and the invasion fizzles out. You can't say, either, that Weiss is a Communist, for he's not. He just gets bad advice."

While Father Ginder's approach is that of the parish priest patiently explaining to his flock, the Reverend Cletus J. Healy, a Jesuit who teaches political science at Marquette High School in Milwaukee, takes the prosecutor's approach. In his loose-leaf paper *The Truth*, done in blue and red ink, Father Healy presents a view, then argues it down.

The Truth has been included in packets distributed at Right-wing seminars, and diocesan newspapers have slipped copies inside as a bonus to readers. Father Healy's position is that Right makes might. He has also been a featured writer in *Our Sunday Visitor*.

Having gone this far, the browser in the Right Wing's

magazine rack becomes intrigued with still other publications. He finds *Don Bell Reports,* a four-page weekly newsletter with a content that stresses political extremism and anti-Semitism. It is sold for $10 a year by the Time For Truth Press in Palm Beach, Florida.

Task Force, an "American Publication for Loyal Americans," is the newsletter of The Defenders of The American Constitution. The society's officers are retired Generals Pedro del Valle and Merritt B. Curtis. The four-page monthly welds political extremism with open anti-Semitism.

There are others, including the *American Nationalist, Counterattack, Inform, Common Sense, Right!,* and the *Dilling Bulletin.* Anti-Semitism and other hate views are mixed with anticommunism. Even Gerald L. K. Smith, thirty-year veteran in the business, was still publishing *The Cross and the Flag* in Los Angeles in 1963.

The Radical Rightist who wants to see views paralleling his own expressed in newspapers finds a few columnists who accommodate. Westbrook Pegler has written: "I have abstained from joining the John Birch Society because it might not be far enough to the right." He said that that movement "may be the first outcry in a grand revolution. . . ." And Washington columnist Holmes Alexander wrote that ". . . Rightists are justifiably angered by attacks upon them for many years by lunatic leftists and more recently by the President of the United States." Alexander also writes for *American Opinion.*

Paul Harvey, American Broadcasting Company commentator, writes a column carried in several papers. Hargis, Schwarz, and Welch recommend him.

Harry Everingham of We, The People! produces a column, too. A recent one defended the arch-Right in the military. "Men like Walker will not remain silent and let their country be betrayed," he wrote. "These are the men we need to lead our military—they are the kind of leaders we need for our boys when they are drafted into service."

Other newspaper columnists include Hargis and Harding's Benson. On another plane is Buckley, who started a weekly column for newspaper syndication shortly after he flayed Welch. The barbed style that helped make his earlier writing successful remains evident in the columns. "The military are being muzzled by the Kennedy administration and the howls of General Walker . . . should not permit us—or the Senate Investigating Committee—to lose sight of the fact," he said in one of them.

Tom Anderson of the Birch Society reaches readers of his *Farm and Ranch* magazine with the column "Straight Talk." A sample:

" 'Better be Red than dead.' That's the new 'national purpose' of the Appeasers. Appeasers are people who feed a crocodile hoping it'll eat them last. Coexistence is immoral. A gutless, impossible delusion and fraud . . .

"Attack us? The communists are not insane enough to attack us. They are winning without it. And they want our cities, our industries, our youth intact. They can win without changing their tactics. We can't win without changing ours."

Anderson's colorful style and pungent language have made him a favorite of unreserved Rightists, especially when he tells of firsthand experiences:

It was at the multi-million-dollar United States embassy building in Stockholm, Sweden. They were having a small cocktail party for our little group accompanying Secretary of Agriculture Benson on a trade development tour. As I joined a group of a dozen or so standing in a circle, one of our embassy employees glibly expounded: "This ain't bad duty now that McCarthy is dead." Quick as you could say Alger Hiss or Phillip C. Jessup, I politely inquired: "How've all you pinks, punks and perverts been getting along since the Senator passed away?" Uninsulted, he answered: "There are just as many of us and we're getting along better than ever."

I don't see how any red-blooded American could mix
with our foreign service and State Department people
without thinking more of Joe McCarthy. Our overseas
employees, like State Department people here, and like
groups anywhere, can't accurately be lumped into one
category. Some are dedicated patriots. Some are One-
Worlders, international socialists, people who've long
since lost their patriotism, if they ever had any. . . . Some
are dupes and do-gooders who are serving the Communist cause unwittingly by following the Communist line.
Some are undoubtedly Communists. Some are merely
gutless traitors. . . . Many of these people, deliberately
or not, are delivering us to the enemy.

Anderson's columns often are reprinted by the Courtneys.

Fulton Lewis, Jr., in print and on the air, is sometimes wary
of the Far Right. Nevertheless, almost every list of recommended reading and listening put out by Ultras includes
Lewis, despite his mild criticisms.

A number of newspapers, scattered across the nation, frequently take editorial positions as far to the Right as those of
any columnist. Some were stirred, for example, by the Walker
affair: The Indianapolis *Star* said: "We welcome, in sadness
for him but with joy for the cause of American Freedom,
Gen. Walker's return to civilian life. What he could not do
under restraints imposed upon him by his timorous superiors
he is now free to do as a citizen of this country we love. We
are certain he will fight for freedom for America. . . ."

The *Arizona Republic:* "In the end, it was General Walker's
insistence on patriotism from his troops . . . that brought
about his downfall. For patriotism—that is, love of one's
country—is unwelcome on the New Frontier, where the
United Nations, and not the U.S., is considered the hope,
and so General Walker was made to pay the penalty."

Manchester (N.H.) *Union Leader:* "In General Walker the

enemy has found a tough and determined opponent. And hopefully he may be the man who will organize and revitalize the literally hundreds of anti-Communist organizations in the United States into an effective fighting force against Communism."

The Charleston (S.C.) *News and Courier:* "In Edwin Walker the people of the United States evidently have a citizen who is mentally and morally prepared to lead the pro-Blue campaign against the Red enemy within."

The Joplin (Mo.) *Globe* warned its readers: "The nation is fairly crawling with Communist spies and agents, thanks in part to extreme civil liberties decisions by the Supreme Court. . . ." The Odessa (Tex.) *American* demanded the impeachment of all members of the Supreme Court "on the grounds that their activities and decisions were in violation of the Constitution and not in the best interests of the individuals in these United States."

One of the most uncompromisingly Right-wing newspapers is the Lima (Ohio) *News*, "an independent freedom newspaper." A letter to the editor signed by Reed Benson said:

"For some time now I have been a great admirer of your newspaper. My father, Ezra Taft Benson, and I are trying to set up a libertarian research center here in Salt Lake and are most anxious to have it supplied with the best of the freedom literature.

"I know this is probably shooting for the stars, but I wonder if there is a possibility that we might get past copies of your newspaper since the Kennedy dynasty came into power. Your editorial page is outstanding and we are most anxious to have it on hand."

The center will be well supplied. The writers of the Far Right are as prolific as those of the Far Left have been.

12:

In Class

"What does it say? What does it say?"

The fifth-grade boys and girls of Lakewood Elementary School in Twin Lakes, Wisconsin, were impatiently curious about the strangest textbook they had ever seen. Some of its pages were pasted over with gummed paper, and the children held them up to the light to read through the layer of brown—without success.

Wives of members of the Twin Lakes school board had sat up nights to make the new textbooks, copies of William Holmes McGuffey's Eclectic Readers of 1879, acceptable in the 1960s—by blotting out religious teachings that might violate the principle of separation of church and state. They had helped to bring the long-outdated McGuffeys back to the schoolroom, thereby complying with the sentiments of a majority of the board's members. It was the majority's feeling that the McGuffey Readers did more to foster such virtues as patriotism and self-reliance than any series currently available.

Revival of the McGuffeys was in conformity with the

board's new statement of "basic principles," which required that "all materials used in our school will constantly be scrutinized in order to avoid indoctrination of our children in socialistic or communistic theories." The statement adds, "Our children will become familiar with the basic documents in their country's history, committing to memory its anthems and pledges, and through regular attention to these and to their meaning will develop an early love for their country."

To quiet the community uproar that followed reintroduction of McGuffey, the board distributed copies of a *Dan Smoot Report* praising the books. The board also reported the receipt of a "flood" of laudatory letters.

"We are sending in two separate packets a bunch of anti-Communist, anti-Socialist literature from various sources," one said. "We felt it would be interesting reading for you who are so obviously Christian Americans.

"Several organizations in the Minneapolis area have been active in showing anti-Communist films through churches, schools and civic and patriotic clubs. The American public is awakening, though slowly, to their immediate peril. Your fight about textbooks adds to the notice to American parents of the control the socialists have over their schools."

The board fired the school principal, Raymond Oestreich, who opposed the swift step back to the century of the McGuffeys. Later he testified that a board member had told him to "burn" or "sell for scrap" some of the books he had been using. Five of the ten teachers on his faculty did not return for a second McGuffey year. One, Mrs. Doris Bannister, said she was told to resign or be fired. She said she was told she did not use the McGuffeys enough.

The turmoil persisted, dividing Twin Lakes, but the board refused to back down and, instead, followed up with an "Americanism Program." This featured reading on the history of the nation designed to "focus the kids' minds on their basic heritage."

William B. Smeeth, clerk of the board and a sparkplug for
its curriculum revisions, has opened a private elementary
school in Brookfield, Wisconsin. As headmaster of this Academy of Basic Education, he hopes to improve upon the shortcomings of public schools, with the help of the McGuffeys.

"Give us the child for eight years," Lenin wrote, "and it
will be a Bolshevik forever. . . ." The Far Right has its own
version of the principle, but its application so far has been
greater at the high school and college level than in elementary schools. The Searcy, Arkansas, National Education Program has had particularly good success in putting its materials to use in high schools in various parts of the country.

America's Future, Inc., nonprofit, tax-exempt "educational"
organization in New Rochelle, New York, has a Textbook
Evaluation Committee that was established to "give this
country its only source of information as to which high school
texts have been infused with un-American ideas intended
to destroy our children's confidence in their nation's form of
government and in its economic system."

The committee has reviewed many of the 400 social-
science textbooks in general use. Its evaluations, which
teachers and school boards receive gratis upon request, disclose the degree to which each text "accurately portrays or
conveys misleading concepts of our government and economic system."

The New Rochelle organization hopes that schools will
take note of its evaluations and adopt texts that do not "dis-
tort our history, disparage our representative form of government, and impute base motives to those who framed our
Constitution."

Further tips to teachers are contained in such pamphlets
as "How Progressive Is Your School?" (*progressive* is a see-
Red word) and Rosalie Gordon's "What's Happened to
Our Schools," described as an account of "the subversion
of schools by Socialist-Communist educators."

Most modern American civics texts, America's Future says, give a great deal of attention to such civil liberties as freedom of religion, speech, and press. It asks: "Is sufficient or equal attention given to other rights, such as the right to acquire and hold property, the right to work, the right to engage in free enterprise, the right of a free society to protect itself against subversion, etc.?"

In many modern economics texts, the organization says, a great deal of space is given to the role which is or should be played by the government in our economy; and it asks "Does the text give sufficient or equal attention to the role played by the private enterpriser in our economy?"

Even standard texts are not immune from attack by the evaluators employed by America's Future. E. Merrill Root, retired professor of English literature at Earlham College and author of *Brainwashing in the High Schools*, reviewed *This Is America's Story*, by Wilder, Ludlum, and Brown, and found it unsatisfactory. He discovered that in describing Andrew Jackson the text used "the unfortunate phrase 'the common man,' a contemporary cliché making 'common' synonymous with virtue." Root, whose name is listed on the stationery of Kent Courtney's Conservative Society of America, also criticized the use of the word *reform* as implying a movement toward something better "rather than often a destruction of something good." According to Root, the text adheres to a double standard by which Nazis are let off easier than Communists. Root found "no Hiss, or Harry Dexter White, or Ware cell, in the index" and concluded that "students are still kept in a timorous hush-hush about the facts of treachery in high places."

Recommendations by the organization are paid some heed. In one state, for example, civic leaders petitioned the governor and legislature to remove as subversive from the approved textbook list not only *This Is America's Story* but also such other standards as *Magruder's American Government*, by McClenaghan; *World History,* by Boak, Slosson, and Anderson; *Geography and World Affairs,* by Jones and Murphy; and *United States History,* by Wirth.

"How Progressive Is Your School" is a checklist offering a "point-by-point comparison of up-to-date traditional education with progressive education for socialism." The pamphlet explains: "the Traditional seeks to educate the mind and build character, to encourage self-reliance and engender a competitive spirit that brings out the best effort each is capable of. The Progressive system submerges the individual in the group and eliminates competition as a spur to initiative. Both its texts and its teachers frequently are critical of free enterprise while they praise planned economy and other socialist doctrine."

In a checklist provided for texts used in elementary schools, social-studies textbooks written along traditional lines are praised as "objective with a degree of nationalistic bias." In progressive schools, on the other hand, "textbooks may be biased, by implication or omission, toward Socialism." "In progressive education," the pamphlet adds, "the objectivity or subjectivity of the teacher is highly significant because unsavory facts about our country, its laws, or its national figures are freely entertained in classroom discussion and may be stressed to an unwarranted degree," while in traditional education "the objectivity or subjectivity of the teacher is not too significant due to 'transfer from text' method."

In "What's Happened to Our Schools?," Miss Gordon rakes progressive education as an effort "to deliberately undereducate our children" so their minds may be molded to accept without question "the subversive political and economic philosophy" of such progressive educators as John Dewey, "a muddle-headed philosopher at Columbia University who was subsequently built up into a kind of leftist god by the collectivists on the campuses of American colleges."

She says "the socialist planners in the educational world"

managed to keep pupils ignorant of their own history and traditions and make them world-minded "through the textbooks used in the progressive system." "A constant stream of propaganda for the United Nations and world government," she goes on to say, "is being fed to the schools by the National Education Association and UNESCO, the specialized propaganda agency of the UN." She assails the National Education Association, the nation's largest organization of teachers, as "pretty tightly controlled at the center by a group of officials who, if not outright leftists, could hardly be described as pro-Americans."

What can parents do to offset this "planned, slyly executed" effort to undereducate their children? Get a copy of "How Progressive Is Your School" and use it as a guide. Join PTAs and try to take them over. Always be on the alert against "any and all attempts to get the hand of the federal government" on the schools. Look into the background and philosophy of school-board members and prospective members. Keep an eye on school libraries to see that progressivist revolutionaries do not "pack them with a preponderance of leftist books." Look at your children's textbooks. "Be eternally vigilant."

The Christian Anti-Communism Crusade has placed its literature in a number of high schools. In Indiana, it helped establish Survival Over Communism, an organization to promote youth study clubs. A manual on how to set up a Survival Club offers a suggested constitution and sample letters to congressmen. Suggested courses of study list Crusade films, tapes, tracts, and books—including Schwarz' *You Can Trust the Communists.*

Three pamphlets from the Crusade were among the first source materials to be included in a bibliography for instruction in communism versus Americanism in a program started by the Dallas Independent School District in 1961. In Houston, weekly meetings of "Teens Against Communism" were held. The Teens, students at Jesse H. Jones High School, had such guest speakers as William Strube, Jr., of the Crusade; on one occasion Strube defined "peaceful co-existence" for them as meaning "total Communist victory." The Teen program was sponsored by an economics teacher at the high school to "arm" students against the dangers of communism and help them understand world affairs.

In Texas and a number of other states it is up to local boards to decide whether schools will teach about communism. Some states have passed laws requiring instruction in all high schools in the differences between communism and the American system. Louisiana was first; it has a mandatory course called "Americanism vs. Communism." Students have viewed films prepared under the auspices of Harding College's National Education Program. A course outline issued by the state superintendent of education in 1961 has a cover picture showing a Russian soldier grabbing the globe while Uncle Sam stands by.

Louisiana teachers were given a six-day summer preparatory course which included a lecture by Schwarz. They were provided materials from several sources, including the House Committee on Un-American Activities. The course stresses praise of the free-enterprise system and presentation of the evils of communism. The syllabus includes such statements as these:

"When Communists negotiate with non-Communists they are not seeking to establish peace, they are seeking to maneuver themselves into the best available position for continuing war."

"Well-meaning but impractical 'do-gooders' and disgruntled intellectuals are often duped into spreading the 'party line.'"

In 1962 Florida made mandatory an annual minimum of thirty hours of high school work on the evils of communism. It laid down these ground rules:

"The course shall be one of orientation in comparative governments and shall emphasize the free-enterprise competitive economy of the United States of America as the one which produces higher wages, higher standards of living, greater personal freedom and liberty than any other system of economics on earth.

"The course shall lay particular emphasis upon the dangers of Communism, the fallacies of Communism, and the false doctrines of Communism."

Barbara Hartle, a Communist Party official in the United States before becoming a speaker on the anti-Communist circuit, said at a Hargis show in Tulsa that such courses should not be objective. Schools should teach "against" communism, she said. She added that she was "not in favor of letting young people decide" for themselves at high school age.

Texans for America, the Haley organization, puts it this way: "The stressing of both sides of a controversy only confuses the young and encourages them to make snap judgments based on insufficient evidence. Until they are old enough to understand both sides of a question, they should be taught only the American side."

Barbara Hartle's view sometimes prevails in current moves to introduce courses in communism and free enterprise. Facts may be presented—so long as they promote an ultraconservative conception of "patriotism." Objective comparisons are considered risky. Encouraging reflective student appraisals is not in the Right-wing program. The result is indoctrination rather than understanding.

In a speech reprinted by America's Future, Max Rafferty, then superintendent of schools of La Canada, California, who was elected state superintendent of public instruction by California voters in 1962, says, "We educators had better not be caught short. We had better not be caught withholding from the nation's children the wonderful sharp-edged, glittering sword of Patriotism. In a word, this means Indoctrination."

The American Bar Association considers this a step in the wrong direction. Neither does it favor the long-prevailing attitude that communism is a subject to be skirted for fear that students might draw "wrong" conclusions. It vigorously supports the need for regular formal instruction at the high school level, but says, "The subject of Communism, like any other subject, should be taught factually, thoroughly and objectively."

This is the conclusion of its Special Committee on Education in the Contrast Between Liberty Under Law and Communism, appointed in 1961 and later incorporated into its Standing Committee on Education Against Communism. After a year of study, the committee warned that special care must be exercised in carrying out such a program "to avoid extremist influence of both the right and left." The committee reported: "Much of the extremism and also the naivete so often found on this subject stems from ignorance and lack of understanding. One of the purposes of this program is to dispel this ignorance, and to focus informed attention on the real enemy of freedom—the international Communist movement and its imminent threat to our country. This must, of course, be done with determination and conviction, but also factually and with due regard to the Bill of Rights and standards of fairness which are the hallmark of the freedom under law we seek to defend."

In a guide for teaching about communism issued in 1962 by a joint committee of the American Legion and the National Education Association, a wholly factual presentation of Communist philosophy and practices was recommended. The guide pointed out that the Communist economic system had scored notable successes and asserted that "it is not necessary to maintain the position that everything about communism is a failure. . . ." It advocated that teaching about communism be handled as part of social-studies courses such as history, geography, and economics, rather than as special courses. Many educators believe that teaching is more likely to deteriorate into propaganda in special courses because the combination of improperly trained teachers and controversial issues results in the teachers' reliance on popular anti-Communist slogans rather than scholarly materials. The recent demand for special courses to teach against communism has been coming from the same groups who opposed any mention of communism in the classroom during the McCarthy era.

Although efforts at teaching an understanding of communism are spreading, many schools are not maintaining the standards urged by either the Bar Association or jointly by the National Education Association and the American Legion. The thoroughness and quality of instruction ranges all the way from ill-prepared, panicky presentations based on Far Right literature to excellent, analytical, and thought-provoking courses prepared with the advice of eminent educators in the field.

The greatest stumbling block everywhere is the lack of junior and senior high school teachers well enough informed about communism to teach it effectively. Where school administrators are determined to remedy this deficiency, desirable changes will come about.

The Pennsylvania Department of Public Instruction, in issuing a guide for a comparative study of democracy and communism in 1960, emphasized that not everyone is capable of leading a class inquiry into the problems of communism. "The teacher is a key factor in such an undertaking," Superintendent of Public Instruction Charles H. Boehm said, "and should not only possess the highest qualifications as a history or social studies teacher, but should be well informed on this subject. The school administrator should give careful thought to the selection of such a person, and then provide adequate materials and instructional aids to assist the teacher. Substitutes, expediencies, and improvised means will not do. The task is very difficult. Careful planning and preparation and much background reading are absolutely necessary. Democratic rather than authoritarian methods are, in the long run, the only ones that will succeed in the classroom. Nothing needs to be distorted or withheld from young, inquiring minds. We must 'practice what we preach.' We should be objective in our approach and seek to learn the facts." Boehm suggested teaching about communism at the twelfth-grade level because seniors were more mature and better prepared than other high school students.

The Chicago school system does this in excellent fashion. A popular elective twelfth-grade course, "Contemporary American History," first offered in 1958 and revised in 1961, compares American institutions with those of communism. The bibliographies list authors from Chester Bowles, Justice William O. Douglas, and Thomas K. Finletter to J. Edgar Hoover, Professor Clinton P. Rossiter, and Clarence B. Randall, former president and chairman of the board of Inland Steel Company. Extremists on both ends of the political spectrum are excluded. As an aid to teachers new to the subject matter, the Chicago Bureau of Curriculum Development included in the program a professional bibliography of recommended books on teaching social studies. The Chicago school system has since been experimenting with a new course on communism and democracy as well.

But teaching about communism, a cold-war development, was still in its infancy in the early 1960s. A 1961 Bar Association survey of 278 communities found few schools teaching the subject. Specific courses on the facts of communism were even missing at the undergraduate level in colleges. Part of the reason has been a desire of school administrators to avoid controversy. Teachers at both levels, even in regular political-science, government, civics, and economics courses, have suffered unusual harassment since the current Far Right movement burgeoned.

Two teachers in Phoenix were forced out of their jobs. One had criticized "Operation Abolition," a Far Right film favorite, and defended the American Civil Liberties Union (to which he belonged) at a PTA meeting. Members of the Birch Society were present and the school board was swamped with demands for the teacher's dismissal.

The other teacher also defended the ACLU at a public meeting and was forced to resign as "too controversial."

A concerted Birch campaign to get the job of another ACLU member in Fullerton, California, failed because the California Teachers Association and the National Education Association's Commission for the Defense of Democracy through Education stepped in to investigate. Their report praised the Fullerton school board and administration for their support of the counselor in the face of the mail and telephone attacks.

Teachers at Southeast High School in Wichita received similar Birch treatment. At the urging of extremists, pupils reported anything said by particular teachers that might be used against them. This became the subject for a barrage of complaints to school authorities from citizens. While the organizers of the complaint campaign failed to oust teachers or alter courses, they created fear and suspicion.

The story was the same at the University of Wichita. As told by George K. Lewis, assistant professor of economics, members of the John Birch Society said openly that they were "out to get" certain instructors. Their efforts to have these teachers discharged have been unsuccessful, he says, because the president of the university, Harry Corbin, rejected the complaints. "But recently," Mr. Lewis remarked in a conversation in 1962, "we have been more insecure. Their efforts are obviously designed to force us clear out."

His own "harassment" stemmed from his stated opposition to "right-to-work" laws and from an article he had written attacking Birchers as extremist. He and others on the faculty who share his views have been called "everything from fellow travelers to Communists," he said.

Lewis said the Birch Society might have no more than 200 members in Wichita but had considerable strength through "association" with business leaders in the Chamber of Commerce.

Delegates to the 1962 convention of the National Education Association were urged to fight back if they were attacked by the Radical Right. A panel of speakers told a session on "Thunder on the Right" that education had much to lose by remaining silent in the face of attack. Joseph Stocker of the Arizona Education Association, reporting on a survey he had conducted on the impact of the Far Right on education, noted that in some communities teachers had lost jobs because of extremists' charges. He said many groups were seeking to impose textbook censorship. Members of the John Birch Society, he reported, were trying to "muscle into" parent-teacher associations and take them over. The "capacity for mischief" of the Radical Right was described as "monumental."

"At the first sign of weakness, submissiveness or appeasement, the ultras only bore in more vigorously," he said. "A weak defense implies guilt, or is so interpreted by the extremists, and it even enables them to win over to their side some of the neutral elements of the community."

Sometimes the charges come from teachers themselves. At Michigan State University, for instance, John N. Moore, associate professor of natural science and an adviser to the campus Conservative Club, said that "socialism is the predominant theory being taught" at Michigan State. And Revilo P. Oliver, the Bircher professor of classics at the University of Illinois, said at a Christian Crusade meeting that college courses on contemporary problems "usually are sheer, pure, unadulterated communism with a little polish on the surface." He told a student questioner, "You are very lucky if you are in a college that has not been infiltrated."

Until he was stopped by his superiors, Everett Shaw, associate professor of business education at Whitewater State College in Wisconsin, showed Right-wing films and passed out extremist pamphlets in his classes. One, published by the Cinema Educational Guild, Inc., of Hollywood, charged that President Kennedy had a nine-year plan to turn the United States over to the United Nations. It called this treason and urged his impeachment.

Because of the Birch Society's extremist reputation, its organizing activities on college campuses have had little success. For example, at the University of California in Santa Barbara, a paid coordinator started a front called the Freedom Club, ostensibly as just another organization of conservative students. But minutes of a meeting of the unit contained the statement that "A further point of attack shall be subtle movements in objectives and use of the Freedom Club so that attention shall not be focused on the actual Society." Exposure by the Santa Barbara *News-Press* finished the Freedom Club.

More successful has been the less extreme Intercollegiate Society of Individualists. Its purpose is to distribute conservative literature to students. At its headquarters on Independence Square in Philadelphia the tax-exempt society has a mailing list of several thousand. Besides flooding campuses with newsletters, monographs, pamphlets, books, and reprints from Philadelphia and regional branch offices, it has held seminars featuring conservatives, arranged speaking tours for Right-wing lecturers, and inspired the creation of student publications. *The Analysis*, publication of the Eleu-

therian Society, an Individualists affiliate at the University
of Pennsylvania, said in its statement of purpose:

> We shall endeavor to effect a change in the thinking of
> the students and faculty of the University of Pennsyl-
> vania to a more conservative outlook.
>
> We shall oppose more government control over the
> life of the individual and shall, in most cases, seek to
> remove governmental influences.
>
> We shall oppose the forces of international and in-
> ternal Communism, which we believe are now the great-
> est single threat to our liberties.
>
> We shall emphasize victory over the Communist ideol-
> ogy rather than mere coexistence with it.

There are many other manifestations of less than Far Right
conservatism at colleges today. The phenomenon is not the
"conservative revolt on the campus" that conservatives pro-
claim, but the trend does show that an increasingly vocal
conservative student minority has been taking a stand in
recent years. One of its fastest-growing elements is the political action group called Young Americans for Freedom,
spawned by the Youth for Goldwater drive at the Republican
National Convention in Chicago in 1960. It was organized
six weeks later at the family home of William Buckley in
Sharon, Connecticut. By 1962 it had more than 21,000 members in college chapters or affiliated directly with the home
office in New York. Beginning in 1961, the organization has
held well-attended annual rallies in Manhattan, each featuring Barry Goldwater.

At the 1962 rally, 18,000 persons paid more than $80,000
to hear Goldwater denounce "the liberal approach to America's problems." Madison Square Garden, decked in red,
white, and blue bunting, was jammed with enthusiastic conservatives, at least half of them students. Signs in crayon pro-

claimed *Rocky No—Barry Yes* and *Staten Island YAF will Vote Goldwater in '64.*

But more bellicose signs were also in evidence: *Hands Off Katanga, Stamp Out Communism, Reds Beware—We Have Had It.* Applause supported L. Brent Bozell, Buckley's brother-in-law, when he stood on the speakers' platform in front of a big slogan reading CONSERVATIVE RALLY FOR WORLD LIBERATION FROM COMMUNISM and demanded a set of "new Orders":

"To the Joint Chiefs of Staff: Prepare for an immediate landing in Havana.

"To the Commander in Berlin: Tear down the wall.

"To our chief of mission in the Congo: Change sides.

"To the chief of the C.I.A.: . . . encourage liberation movements" in every nation under communism.

M. Stanton Evans, young editor of the Indianapolis *News,* wrote in *Revolt on the Campus* that the student conservative "believes the nature of the adversary is such that we cannot coexist with it, but must defeat it, if we are to survive."

Although these conservatives are but a small percentage of the total college enrollment, their viewpoint and that of the Ultras who may influence them has become a cause of concern to many educators. Before the current movement even got into high gear, Professor Richard Hofstadter of Columbia University, in an essay on the Rightists, called them "pseudo-conservatives." Some have more in common with ex-General Walker and the "fight now" element than with Barry Goldwater, who confines his belligerence to a vaguer "policy of victory."

13:

On Base

> One of the easiest ways of determining your Senator's or Congressman's record is by consulting the ACA Index. This carefully researched index to voting records has been prepared by the nonpartisan Americans for Constitutional Action. A copy of this is available to all. You can phone Flak M813 to have your representative's records determined before your vote is cast. When the American public understands the relationship of congressional voting records to national security, the cause of freedom will be revitalized.

So advised the column "Commanding General's Notebook" in the October 8, 1960, issue of *Taro Leaf*, newspaper of the American 24th Infantry Division in the 2000-year-old city of Augsburg, Germany.

The commanding general was Edwin A. Walker, member of the John Birch Society from Center Point, Texas. Flak Military 813 was the telephone number of a "special projects office" he had established at his headquarters earlier in the year. The voting information it had for the troops was that

compiled by the ultraconservative ACA under these "indexes":
"consistency"; "for sound money and against inflation"; "for
economy and conservatism and against waste"; "for private-
competitive market and against government interference";
"for local self-government and against central government intervention"; "for private ownership and against government
ownership and control of the means of production and distribution"; "for individual liberty and against coercion"; and
"national security."

Besides offering his men counsel in determining which
candidates back home to vote for, Walker addressed them
and their dependents on the perils of Communist subversion.
He also invited other speakers of similar persuasion to address his troops, including William Schlamm, associate editor
of *American Opinion* and Edgar Bundy, author of *Collectivism in the Churches.*

Walker, much-decorated veteran of World War II and the
Korean War, also recommended for reading and distributed
to company and battery-size units in his division Welch's
The Life of John Birch. All of this was part of a "pro-blue"
troop education and indoctrination program established by
Walker in 1960.

According to a 24th Division information spokesman,
Walker called his program *pro-blue* "because blue has the
symbolic meaning of loyalty." Blue is at the opposite end of
the spectrum from red. Billy James Hargis, in his *Weekly
Crusader,* explains Walker's use of the term this way:

"A staff officer was commenting on a map which showed
Communist countries in red and America and her allies in
blue. The officer referred to the free world as 'anti-red.'
'That's defensive thinking,' Walker responded. 'We're pro-
blue.' This is the way in which General Walker named the
pro-blue program for his 24th Infantry Division in Augsburg,
Germany."

Whatever its inspiration, the program was too flagrant for

the Pentagon. An investigation was ordered and the acting Inspector General of the Army, Lieutenant General Frederic J. Brown, found the Walker program and that of the John Birch Society "remarkably identical." The Army's investigation found that Walker had conducted a troop indoctrination program that overstepped Army regulations "by making speeches containing remarks that were inflammatory and derogatory to past public officials, quoting and recommending material which was in varying degrees nonfactual, biased and inflammatory in character, and arranging for speakers who gave inflammatory speeches." It also found that Walker, "acting in an official capacity, attempted to influence the members of the 24th Infantry Division and their dependents in their selection of senatorial and congressional candidates by recommending the use of voting materials not obtained through military sources."

Walker was admonished and relieved of his command in a scheduled transfer. He resigned from the Army to be free to express his views in the political arena.

From the moment he held his first news conference, it was obvious to all but his fellow Far Rightists that he was badly miscast as a politician. The big, dark, powerful, well-groomed bachelor, fit and trim in his early fifties, made an imposing figure—until he opened his mouth. Then the picture changed as the result of his halting, stumbling, suspicious, defiant, sometimes inarticulate responses to questions. The answers were uncompromising Welch, and the verbal excesses matched those of Welch. Many conservatives who had hoped he would be an effective spokesman for freeing military officers to speak out against communism were disappointed.

Walker launched his political career in the sparkling Arie Crown Theatre in McCormick Place, Chicago's new convention hall on Lake Michigan, on the chilly night of February 9, 1962. The overwhelmingly Right-wing crowd of 5000 was excited. Soon to step from the wings of the vast stage was the man who had ignored warnings from associates and superiors and defied the government with an indoctrination program that had cost him his command in Germany. He had spent three decades in uniform and had been decorated for a valiant battle against Communists in Korea. Ever since he had left the prosperous Walker family ranch in Center Point and had been graduated low in the West Point class of 1931, he had had a fighting career. A colonel in World War II, he had commanded the paratroopers and commandos of a Canadian-American special service force in Italy, France, and Germany. In Korea he had fought to Heartbreak Ridge, to be halted by what he considered inexcusable political compromise. The Far Right was delighted with his report that the "stalemate" accepted in Korea had prompted his personal investigation of the internal Communist threat and had led him into the John Birch Society in 1959, the first year it was open to membership. Since then he had spent some $10,000 of his own money to provide anti-Communist literature for his troops in Germany. Especially convincing to the Far Right of Walker's deadly seriousness about their mission, he had resigned from the Army to work for the Cause unimpeded, forfeiting more than $12,000 a year he would have received had he simply retired.

When the Movement's chief martyr parted the curtains and strode, ramrodstraight, to the center of the stage, the crowd rose and cheered. Armed, uniformed Legionnaires marched onto the platform to post the colors. The newest hero of the Far Right leaned over the rostrum to open his first drive for political office:

"It may seem unusual to launch a campaign for Governor of Texas in Chicago," he said in his flat, deep drawl, "but after what has happened to me for the past year, nothing is unusual." For the next ninety minutes, interrupted often by hearty applause and once by a heckler, the ex-general read a diatribe against the government and democratic institutions that could have come directly from the Birch Society's Blue Book.

For 20 years the United States government has acted as if it were an agent of the Soviet Union, he asserted. "We saw to it that the Communists had an opportunity to take over China, we saw to it that their ally Red China acquired prestige for a victory in Korea, at a time when we were the acknowledged Number One power of the world."

"The most shocking example of our collaboration with Soviet Russia," the dark-visaged ex-commander went on, "is in the field of nuclear and space technology. . . . Information and materials were furnished Soviet Russia systematically on instructions from top Government levels. . . ." Part of the result, he added, has been Russian space achievements of great propaganda value. "This effect has been largely created by the American press," he said.

The "left-wing press sellout of America" came in for frequent mention. So did subversion in higher places. U.S. government policy, Walker declared, "has undermined the morale of NATO and participated in actions subversive thereto. Our entire NATO set-up, so fabulously expensive, is never permitted to interfere with what the Soviets want. . . . NATO now exists on Communist sufferance and will be liquidated on Communist signal. . . ."

"With devious intent," Walker added, "the sure effect of NATO has been to limit the exercise of sovereignty and independent power in all Western countries. . . . NATO's first Commander, General Eisenhower, said in *Crusade in Europe:* 'The democracies must learn that the world is now too small for the rigid concepts of national sovereignty. . . .' Yet one-worlders who preach the relinquishment of some of our sovereignty always show respect for the Russian insistence on complete Soviet sovereignty." He assailed what he called Eisenhower's "Camp David Coexistence Crusade" and noted that the former President had been "pleased" to set foot on

Lenin's tomb in Moscow. He quoted him as saying in Berlin after World War II that "overshadowing all goals for us Americans was the contribution we might locally make toward establishing a working partnership between the United States and Russia." The Texan concluded, "It is no wonder that General Eisenhower does not approve of the superpatriots opposing Communism."

President Kennedy was unceremoniously lumped with his predecessor: "Kennedy has never done anything so dramatic as standing on top of Lenin's tomb, but his stroll through the garden with Khrushchev in Vienna last June was evidence of a desire to walk as far as possible with the Soviets."

Walker used Welch's "Tower of Babel" to describe the United Nations and demanded that the United States pull out of "this unholy alliance with the enemies of God and man" unless the Soviet Union and its satellites did. "We have a policy of submitting to the United Nations," he said, "and in the United Nations the Soviet Union has a veto."

He defended his troop-indoctrination program in words that have been picked up by the Extreme Right all over the country: ". . . my pro-blue training program was not designed to facilitate good relations with the enemy or good relations between free America and the dictatorship in Moscow. Pro-blue was designed to make the men of my command the best possible soldiers for the United States of America, and to give them an understanding of why they had to be in Germany facing the Communist conspiracy. I presumed they had to be there to defend the United States against communism. It appears that from the government's point of view I was wrong."

The soldier-turned-politician did not neglect the domestic issue that concerns the Far Right most, the growing role of the federal government in areas once handled by the states. "The States of our Union are not provinces," he said, "though left-wing collectivists would like to make them so. The obliteration of State lines is high on the agenda of Communists, their fellow travelers, and other zealots of centralism."

But his main emphasis was *superpatriotism*—a word he used proudly several times—and he attacked the administration for what seemed to him a drifting "twilight course of action." To the cheers of the crowd he shouted, "In patriotism, loyalty and combat there are no moderates. People read the moderate propaganda of the day because that is all they can get, but they do not like it. In fact, they are getting indignant about it." He called on the 5000 to "attack on all fronts," and he ordered each to "Man your weapon and speak boldly!"

The audience responded with appreciation. Other audiences to follow did the same. Ultras turned out by the thousands to cheer him on in Texas. But Ted Walker, a good and experienced field general, was simply not a politician. His quick shift to the campaign trail, against formidable competition, was bumpy. His limited, ultraconservative point of view, his lack of depth and interests and experience, and his inarticulateness in off-the-cuff, on-the-record repartee hurt his ambitions despite the vigor of his efforts. By the time of the Texas primary in May 1962 it was no surprise that he should run last in a field of six Democrats. It was more surprising that he received the votes of 138,000 Texans. He had delivered his own *coup de grace* in the forum that presented his greatest opportunity. In two days of testimony, April 4 and 5, 1962, before a special Senate preparedness subcommittee investigating Senator Thurmond's allegations that the military was being "muzzled" in its attempts to fight communism in the cold war, the embittered ex-general made so many unfounded statements about national policymakers and presented his case in such a reckless, disorganized, stumbling manner that he discredited his cause in the eyes of all but the ultraconservatives.

Walker told the Senators that a "hidden control apparatus"

of the government was dictating a "no-win" policy toward the global Communist conspiracy. Although *no-win* is a term frequently used by Senator Thurmond and others of the Right Wing in describing administration policy, no responsible conservative has imputed traitorous motives to the cold-war policies of the government. Walker did. He linked Secretary of State Dean Rusk and Walt Whitman Rostow, head of the State Department's Policy Planning Council, to a conspiratorial "control apparatus," a mysterious entity which he said would "not tolerate militant anti-Communist leadership by a division commander." He described himself as a "scapegoat" of the apparatus' "unwritten policy of collaboration and collusion with the international Communist conspiracy which has superseded all written directives."

Pressed to explain his charges against Rusk and Rostow, the ex-general replied haltingly that the Secretary of State was on General Joseph (Vinegar Joe) Stilwell's staff "during the agrarian reform highlights of that day."

"He was a member and supporter of the Institute of Pacific Relations, which was greatly influenced by Owen Lattimore," Walker added. General Stilwell commanded American troops in China and Burma during World War II. The mention of Lattimore recalled the days of McCarthyism.

Walker also mentioned other old names—none of men ever convicted of anything. His efforts to pinpoint current Communist conspiracy were weak. When asked if he had anyone in mind besides Rusk, he said: "Mr. Walter Rostow, Walt —I believe it is Rostow—who have been in control of the operating arm of C.I.A., I believe, since 1954."

Rusk said the charges were "not worthy of comment." Even Thurmond, agreeing with some of Walker's views, condemned his "methods." Many Rightists were dismayed with the performance.

Walker even remained unintelligible when Senators sought to explore seriously his views on how to combat the Communist threat. When asked what he meant by the "real control apparatus," he said: "The real control apparatus can be identified by its effects and what it is doing, what it did in Cuba, what it is doing in the Congo, what it did in Korea. All these things were done by people. . . . So the apparatus is in those who wanted to see these things happen, and the propaganda front they are using for this and the means to do it with is the United Nations, which is the nearest thing to the Tower of Babel that has ever been built."

Senator E. L. Bartlett of Alaska asked if he should infer that this meant some persons of leadership in the government were sinister anti-Americans seeking to sell out the country. "That is correct, yes, sir," Walker replied. "When you refer to 'sell-out' as a sell-out of our traditions, our Constitution, our sovereignty, our independence, this is correct."

Walker also assailed President Kennedy, former President Eisenhower, Secretary of Defense Robert S. McNamara and two of his assistants, Mrs. Franklin D. Roosevelt, and others. His statements were so discursive and couched in such garbled syntax that the Senators, who treated him with courtesy and patience, sometimes tried to help with a friendly, "What are you saying, General?"

The Texan had brought along two aides, who sought by scribbled notes and whispered advice to keep their charge on the track. They were Clyde J. Watts, a retired brigadier general who practices law in Oklahoma City, and Medford Evans of the Conservative Society of America and the John Birch Society. There was little they could do to keep Walker's chin from quivering with emotion as he testified or to keep his voice from rising in anger from time to time. But possibly because of their advice, Walker did not repeat conspiracy charges to newspapermen outside the hearing room. Only at the hearing was he legally privileged from prosecution. When Tom Kelly, five-foot-five, 155-pound reporter for the Wash-

ington *Daily News,* tried to ask him in the corridor outside
whether he disavowed the support of George Lincoln Rockwell, who had attended the hearing until he was ejected for
wearing a lapel swastika, the six-foot, 200-pound Walker
caught Kelly in the left eye with a right jab and walked on
without a word.

Walker was not able to explain what he would consider
a "win" policy for the United States. He charged that there
was an unwritten policy of collaboration and collusion with
the international Communist conspiracy that had "paralyzed"
the armed forces. He also charged that some books in the
troop information program approved for the Army "implicitly
encourage accommodation with the enemy—competitive
coexistence."

If competitive coexistence is collaboration, then all the
nation's top leaders since World War II have been collab-
orationists. Competitive coexistence, the American majority
and its leaders are convinced, is far preferable to the alternative of nuclear war. The nation's cold-war policy, considered spineless by Walker, is to contain communism by
adequate defense measures while seeking to outstrip the
enemy economically and politically so that the freedom of
the Western world may prevail. Walker's contributions at the
hearing to a better policy amounted to less than zero because
even his points on collaboration and accommodation went
unexplained and unproved.

A clue to the fuzziness of Walker's thinking was given in
his charges about the books. Ever since World War II, he
said, the Army troop information program had been "uncertain." He cited its reading-program list for 1960 as including books by Harry and Bonaro Overstreet, Max Lerner,
John Gunther, and Walter Millis. He said that all of these
and others on the list encouraged competitive coexistence.
But he astonished observers the next day when he conceded,

under questioning, that he had never read any of the books he attacked. He said he had read some reviews and had heard discussions of them.

Walker expressed his feeling, shared by some other commanding officers and by Right-wing civilians, that "the traditional civilian control of the military has been perverted and extended into a commissar-like system of control at all major echelons of command." He again defended his pro-blue program as preferable to the official troop information programs, which he described as "unorganized, improperly manned, unfinanced and uncoordinated for an adequate effort to provide the necessary cold war training" for the armed forces.

Actually, a vast amount of pamphlets, booklets, films, and other material make up the Pentagon's Troop Information and Education Program. This material seeks to make complicated ideological and international questions simple enough for soldiers and sailors of limited education and experience to grasp. The material is slanted to neither Left nor Right, but is couched in terms that are adequate and appropriate to the subject matter of communism, democracy, and the cold war. Although all of the officially approved material is available to the separate services and commands, along with approved reading lists, execution of an information and education program for troops at any post is a function of the command level of that post. Only when such programs have been given a political coloration by commanding officers has Secretary McNamara applied the governing principle of civilian control. Following the Walker case, a Pentagon directive resulted in returning to junior officers, who have more direct contact with troops, more of the responsibility of indoctrination.

All the turmoil on this subject can be traced to the rise of the Far Right movement.

The Walker story, whose denouement came with the former general's arrest on federal charges, later dropped, of seditious conspiracy and inciting insurrection at the University of Mississippi at the time of the enrollment of the first Negro there, is an extreme but not an isolated case of military involvement with the Radical Right. The former general is only one of a number of high-ranking officers who in recent years have encouraged views resembling those of the John Birch Society.

Their indoctrination programs, which have sometimes criticized and ridiculed the government and its policies, took various forms. Some showed troops such movies as the House Un-American Activities Committee's "Operation Abolition," a film much criticized for depicting student rioting against committee hearings in San Francisco as entirely Communist-inspired and Communist-led. Other commanders branched out beyond the base, directing some of their attention to the general public in nearby communities. Programs sponsored, cosponsored, participated in, or otherwise abetted by military commanders have taken the form of seminars, "alerts," "freedom forums," schools on anticommunism, and "strategy-for-survival conferences." Some were held on base, others off. Commanders spoke at some, simply sat on the platform at others. The projects often had a strong Right-wing slant, featuring Fringe speakers and showings of "Operation Abolition" and "Communism on the Map." Many leaders of the Far Right are retired officers of high rank who share the aggressive orientation of brothers in uniform and, their active duty over, feel unrestrained in expressing their convictions.

The point most forcefully made at the Rightist-oriented seminars was that Communist internal subversion and influence was rife in the United States, as seen in social-welfare and foreign-aid programs and willingness to coexist on the globe with Communists. Civilians "alerted" at such functions often were urged to follow through by forming or joining neighborhood groups to alert more of the citizenry to the possibilities of subversive influence in their blocks, schools, libraries, newspapers, and governing bodies.

Military involvement in such adventures has been scattered but nationwide. A series of "strategy-for-survival" conferences was held in Fort Smith, Fayetteville, and Little Rock, Arkansas. In a report placed in the *Congressional Record* by Senator Fulbright, Major General William C. Bullock, the area commander, is said to have persuaded the armed services committee of the Little Rock Chamber of Commerce to sponsor the Little Rock meeting. The report said: "Attendance was pushed through both the Arkansas National Guard and the Reserve units. Through this activity the meetings and information disseminated had in the public eye the stamp of approval of the Army and National Government."

Speakers included President Benson and Vice-President Clifton L. Ganus, Jr., of Harding College. The report said that at the Fort Smith meeting Ganus made the statement that "your Representative in this area has voted 89 per cent of the time to aid and abet the Communist Party." A speaker at all three conferences was Robert Morris, who discussed "No Wonder We Are Losing" and "We Are Losing from Within."

Harding College also had a prominent role in "Project Alert," a civilian-military effort in a number of cities to warn the citizenry of the Communist peril. This elaborate undertaking, initiated late in 1959 at Lubbock, Texas, had perhaps its greatest flowering in a series of community activities in Pensacola, Florida, in 1960 and 1961, when Vice-Admiral Robert Goldthwaite was chief of naval air training at Pensacola. Before the project started, Admiral Goldthwaite and members of his staff had gone to Harding College to examine the "methods the college was using in teaching Americanism." The Naval Air Station also flew National Education Program speakers to Pensacola. When Pensacola's "Project Alert" began, Harding material was disseminated and used

for rallies, seminars, and broadcasts. Admiral Goldthwaite
served as a member of the project's executive committee.

Persons attending "Project Alert" seminars received "cold-
war information packets" recommending, in a what-can-I-do
list, the showing of "Operation Abolition" and "Communism
on the Map." Also recommended were such books as *The
Naked Communist* and such magazines as *American Mercury*
and *American Opinion*. Sources of information suggested included Christian Crusade, the National Education Program,
and the Cardinal Mindszenty Foundation. The packets also
contained this exhortation: "Demand of the President of the
United States, the Secretary of State, the Senate Foreign
Relations Committee, and your representatives in Congress
that our nation immediately establish a foreign policy based
on Godly moral principles and supporting freedom for all
mankind—to replace the policy of 'co-existence with evil.'
Demand that our nation take the offensive in the 'Cold War'
with the objective of victory over Communism. . . ."

Invitations to attend lectures at the station by Ganus and
Glenn Green had gone out on Navy stationery. They said:
"In order to make you and your family aware of the extent
and how hard the Communists are working right this very
moment to take away our freedom and our American way of
life, which so many of us take for granted, a group of civilian
supervisors, as a part of the Pensacola Navy Civilian Leadership Program, has arranged for you, my fellow supervisor
and American, a very special and most important presentation on Saturday, 20 October at 0830, in the Naval Air Station main auditorium, Building 633. If, when you enter the
Main Gate of the Naval Air Station, you will follow the
Awake Survival signs, you cannot miss the location."

Similar to "Project Alert" was "Project Action," the name
given a seminar held at the Naval Air Station in Minneapolis.
The station made overnight accommodations available to
participants for fifty cents each. "The purpose of Project
Action," the official announcement said, "is to inspire the

citizens of this area to take an active part in the war against
the danger that threatens our freedom and American way of
life. The program of talks and presentations by nationally
known leaders for the cause of Democracy will bring to light
facts and figures concerning the rising crime rate, juvenile
delinquency, drug addiction, the general degradation of
morale, the complacent attitude toward patriotism and the
tremendous gains the Communist conspiracy is making in
this country. . . ."

A "Fourth-Dimensional Warfare Seminar" was sponsored
in Pittsburgh in 1961 by its Chamber of Commerce in cooperation, the announcement said, with various military organizations in the area. "Operation Abolition" was shown
and suggestions about "What You Can Do in the Fight
against Communism" were made. The tips included: "Be on
the alert for Communist sympathizers in your community,
especially those who can mold youth or public opinion. . . .
Identify public officials and policies displaying softness
toward communism. Demand a more patriotic attitude. Be
wary of films which stress social and moral depravity. Moral
and social subversion are recognized operational methods of
the Communist Party to weaken the moral fiber of this Nation." Reserve officers received training credit for attendance.
The seminar staff thanked Lieutenant General Ridgely
Gaither, commanding general of the Second Army, and Major
General Ralph C. Cooper, commanding general of the 21st
U.S. Army Corps, and their staffs for their "assistance and
support."

At Corpus Christi, Rear Admiral Louis J. Kirn, Chief of
Naval Air Advanced Training there, sat on the platform during "Citizens Alert Day in Corpus Christi." The main speaker
was William Strube of the Christian Anti-Communism Crusade.

The Crusade has had military aid in staging a number of
its seminars. Schwarz held a "freedom forum" in Houston at
which Rear Admiral F. B. Warders, commandant of the

Eighth Naval District, gave the keynote address. At New
Orleans, headquarters of the district, a Schwarz meeting was
endorsed by Rear Admiral W. G. Schindler in these terms:
"I am delighted to lend my support to this noteworthy
seminar."

In the summer of 1960 Schwarz was in Glenview, Illinois,
where citizens received franked Navy envelopes containing
this message: "The U.S. Naval Air Station, Glenview, Ill.,
presents 'Education for American Security.'" The education
was presented at an auditorium on the station for five days to
audiences of base personnel, reservists, and civilians from the
area. The announced purpose was "to motivate an active
force against moral decay, political apathy and spiritual
bankruptcy, and to bring an awareness of the ominous hammer and sickle that threaten the very life of our nation."
Captain Isaiah M. Hampton, self-styled "Texas conservative"
then in command at the station, welcomed registrants at the
opening session. Speakers besides Schwarz included E. Merrill Root, Herbert Philbrick, and Richard Arens.

The program was planned by Lieutenant Commander
Charles Bigler, intelligence officer at the base, and Francis
J. Vignola, furniture dealer in nearby Forest Park, an air
reservist. The event, Vignola said, was held under Captain
Hampton's "inspiration." In addition to the announcement
that went out to civilians, a notice was received by Navy
personnel and their families. "Attendance is not compulsory,"
it said, "but every man, woman and student who volunteers
participation will acquire the experience, poise, and know-
how which we hope will germinate into discussion groups
being organized in every community of the Midwest."

As with other Schwarz seminars, the Glenview program
did have wide-ranging repercussions. The Glenview Village
Board passed a resolution commending the venture. Local
anti-Communist study organizations were set up, one by
Naval Reserve officers. A few enlisted men from the nearby
Great Lakes Naval Training Center, similarly inspired, took

upon themselves the task of traveling, even outside the state, on week ends to spread the alarm. Since that seminar they have addressed thousands of Midwesterners and have shown "Operation Abolition" in living rooms, school assembly halls, and service-club rooms—working on their own time, in civilian clothes.

The seminar also spurred dissension and complaints. The American Civil Liberties Union sent a protest to the Secretary of the Navy arguing that it was improper "for the commanding officer of the base to conduct such a school, for another naval officer to direct it, or for the Navy to attempt to influence public opinion of the general civilian public on moral, spiritual, educational and political issues." Dr. Tyler Thompson, professor of religion at Northwestern University, wired the Secretary: "I wish to protest the apparent official link of the Navy to the political propaganda being disseminated at the Education for American Security at Glenview Naval Air Station. Official program and early publicity clearly indicate Naval sponsorship. Please investigate." The result was a denial of direct Navy sponsorship. However, the Defense Department, in a letter responding to a query from Senator Clifford Case of New Jersey, said that "when it was determined that officials of the Naval Air Station were going further than was considered appropriate in cooperating with the sponsors of this event," the Navy instructed the commander of the station to cease using naval personnel to promote it.

Few would disagree that such seminars tend to give an air of military sponsorship when uniformed officers of high rank are in visible and prominent presence. But commanders whose views prompt them to encourage or take part in such activities sometimes justify themselves by citing service directives which implement a classified statement of policy that was evolved by the National Security Council in 1958. This generalized policy statement called for use of all the resources of the government, including the military, to strengthen the "cold war" effort on all fronts. The implementing orders, also classified, called on commanders to alert not only their troops but the public to the issues of national security. The individual commanders were left wide latitude in applying the directives.

This loose control of the flammable mixture of politics and the military prompted, in 1961, a memorandum from Senator Fulbright to the Secretary of Defense. It pointed out that a number of seminars "closely identified with military personnel" had made use of "extremely radical right wing speakers and/or materials, with the probable net result of condemning foreign and domestic policies of the Administration in the public mind." Running through all these programs, the memorandum said, "is a central theme that the primary, if not exclusive, danger to this country is internal Communist infiltration." It added:

> Past and current international difficulties are often attributed to this, or ascribed to "softness," "sellouts," "appeasements," etc. Radical Right-wing speakers dominate the programs. . . . The thesis of the nature of the Communist threat often is developed by equating social legislation with socialism, and the latter with communism. Much of the administration's domestic legislative program, including continuation of the graduated income tax, expansion of social security (particularly medical care under social security), Federal aid to education, etc., under this philosophy, would be characterized as steps toward communism.
>
> This view of the Communist menace renders foreign aid, cultural exchanges, disarmament negotiations, and other international programs as extremely wasteful, if not actually subversive. This is a most moderate characterization.

Whether these instances are representative of programs implementing the National Security Council directive is not known, but the pattern they form makes it strongly suspect that they are. There are many indications that the philosophy of the programs is representative of a substantial element of military thought, and has great appeal to the military mind. A strong case can be made, logically, that this type of activity is the inevitable consequence of such a directive. There is little in the education, training or experience of most military officers to equip them with the balance of judgment necessary to put their own ultimate solutions—those with which their education, training, and experience are concerned—into proper perspective in the President's total strategy for the nuclear age. If the military is infected with this virus of Right-wing radicalism, the danger is worthy of attention. If it believes the public is, the danger is enhanced. If, by the process of the military "educating" the public, the fevers of both groups are raised, the danger is great indeed.

The memorandum suggested that the cold-war policy of the 1958 directive be reconsidered. Shortly afterward, McNamara forbade military officials to express views that were politically partisan or contrary to established national policy at programs sponsored by groups outside the government. He said they could speak at such programs if their participation "does not lend an air of sponsorship to the statements of others which may be either partisan in character or contrary to established national policy." McNamara also forbade the use of military facilities or personnel for such programs unless the seminars were sponsored by responsible organizations and there was no reason to believe the views to be expressed would be partisan or contrary to national policy. He banned sponsorship or co-sponsorship of such affairs by any military unit unless it was expressly authorized by the

Secretary of a military department. But he left with local commanders the responsibility for deciding whether seminars planned by outside groups met his criteria for military participation.

While the new Defense Department directive, issued late in 1961, has had a restricting effect on the freedom of military officers to advocate Right-wing theories or support them at public functions, it is far from ironclad. But the administration believes that the restrictions, along with the example of the Walker case, will serve as guidance to those commanders who are inclined to interpret the 1958 directive as license to indulge in any form of superpatriotism. There is some evidence to suggest that the restrictions have caused near-apoplexy among some of the leaders of the Far Right. Welch, for example, calls the crackdown "Operation FIB" (Fulbright Intimidation Binge). Walker says commanders "are leaning over backward not to stick their necks out."

The Defense Department does not oppose seminars on communism that meet its standards for responsibility. Far from it. The Industrial College of the Armed Forces sends a team of officers to a dozen or so cities a year to conduct seminars for reservists and for invited members of the general public. In addition, the facilities of the National War College at Fort McNair in Washington, the services' highest educational institution, are used each summer for "national strategy seminars" which are conducted for reserve officers. A primary aim is to inspire the participants, after two weeks of briefing on the state of the cold war, to return home and organize seminars for the dissemination of the information they received.

The Fulbright memorandum questioned the tone of the War College seminars as well as the flagrantly Rightist forums staged at some military bases. The Senator asked whether the views presented at the War College seminars were too aggressive to be in line with national policy. Testifying in the crowded marble caucus room of the old Senate

Office Building, McNamara said that the point was not well taken. His assistants, he said, had compared the War College seminars with others and had reached this conclusion: "There are several different types of seminars, from thought-provoking, well-guided, informative affairs to extreme right-wing, witch-hunting, mudslinging revivals. Some are profitable discussions with differing points of view reflecting the free exchange of opinion essential to a democracy; others are bigoted, one-sided presentations advocating that the danger to our security is internal only, and that foreign aid and other facets of Administration policy are unnecessary excrescences. They preach adoption of methods similar to those of the Communists."

His report said "the basically responsible group of seminars" centered on the work of the Institute for American Strategy, a private educational corporation headquartered in Chicago, and the Foreign Policy Research Institute of the University of Pennsylvania. Both have had key roles in sponsorship and direction of the War College seminars, as well as in others. McNamara also singled out Frank R. Barnett, since early 1963 director of the National Strategy Information Center in New York City, for special credit.

In an address at a War College seminar in 1961, Barnett gave the reserve officers some advice on how to insure that seminars they might form did not deteriorate into the "cockle-doodle" variety. "There are cockle-doodle seminars for an understandable reason," he said. "Our country is alarmed about Communism. The people feel we have suffered reverses over a period of fifteen years in the cold war. The people are frustrated, and frustration often leads to injudicious action. Some of these offbeat seminars may suggest that the answer to the Communist problem—and I'm overstating the case—is to be found in discovering a fellow traveler in one's own PTA. This solution is an easy psychological outlet for deep frustrations. It enables people to think they are do-

ing their duty by God and country 'on the cheap,' because, if
the problem is almost exclusively one of internal subversion,
then, of course, we don't have to think about the challenge of
Soviet solid-fuel missiles, or strengthening NATO, or improv-
ing foreign-aid management, or volunteering for the Peace
Corps, or anything else that might require sacrifice and a
shift of energy from business as usual. All we have to do is
worry about some 'pinko' in a teacher's college. If you do
organize a seminar at the grass-roots level, the most important thing to bear in mind is the need for quality control. In
other words, if a local college or university, plus a labor
union, plus half a dozen other groups representing the spectrum of professions in the community, all co-sponsor, almost
automatically your program committee (representing all
these groups) will select speakers and materials which are
acceptable. Seminars sponsored by only one group may possibly lack the kind of quality control and consensus needed."

Despite the advice, even a few of the seminars sparked by
War College indoctrination and the Industrial College of the
Armed Forces have gone astray. Barnett winces at such setbacks and continues to preach "quality control." Off the dais,
the former Rhodes Scholar and lifelong student of foreign
policy and military strategy describes himself as a "Taft Republican." He concedes his consuming interest in alerting the
public to the long-term dangers of what he sees as a "pro-
tracted" cold-war conflict. The West must be prepared, he
says, to meet the enemy on every front—psychological, economic, and scientific as well as military. But there is a
notable absence of hysteria in the resonant voice of the
much-traveled Illinoisan. He denounces those of the Radical
Right who equate social-welfare legislation with Communism.

Barnett, who studied at Wabash College and the Universities of Syracuse, California, and Zurich as well as at Oxford,
participates in scores of "strategy" seminars and conferences

in addition to those held at the War College. One continuing series he endorses highly is conducted in cities throughout the country by the American Bar Association's Committee on Education Against Communism, formerly its Committee on Communist Tactics, Strategy and Objectives. He told a seminar of the committee in St. Louis in 1962 that there had been far too much talk about the internal threat of communism in this country. "The way to combat Communist propaganda is not to set one's self up in competition with the FBI," he said, but to do enough "homework" on Communist strategy and objectives to become informed. He warned against heeding "random and uninformed pressure groups." Such responsible programs as those of the Bar Association's committee helped fill an informational vacuum the Far Right had leapt into without, for a time, much effective challenge.

Rear Admiral William C. Mott, Judge Advocate General of the Navy and a member of the bar committee, says "amateur anti-Communists" are as useful as "amateur brain surgeons" when allowed to participate in public affairs seminars. "We have no need for space-age witch hunters," he told the Senate subcommittee investigating Pentagon reins on the military.

The surge of denunciation of the methods of the Far Right has played a part in influencing the military commanders inclined to use the 1958 directive to play footsie with the extremists. Officers also have seen the new handwriting of the Kennedy administration between the lines of the directive. With the Walker case and the nationwide hubbub in mind, they apparently have felt constrained to remember that their role in a civilian-directed government calls for distinguishing between military and political questions. As McNamara testified: "The military establishment is an instrument—not a shaper—of national policy. Its members—as free Americans —are entitled to their views on the issues of the day, and they have every right to try to make their views effective through the ballot. They do not have the right, however, to use the military establishment to advance partisan concepts or to alter the decisions of the elected representatives of the people."

The reminder was overdue. Concern had grown that a belligerent and free-wheeling military could conceivably become as dangerous to the stability of the United States as the mixture of military rebelliousness and politics had in nations forced to succumb to juntas or fascism. The agony that gripped France as a result of military defectors' efforts to reverse government policy on Algeria was another forceful reminder of the inherent dangers in allowing political power to build up in the military establishment.

Yet the Fringe cannot be expected to drop its valuable links to the prestigious American military establishment without a struggle. This association has been one of the Radical Right's most useful assets. Throughout the period of uproar the Ultras have seized every opportunity to capitalize on association with respected men of rank. All are heroes who can be of aid to the messianic leaders on the Far Right on their road to self-aggrandizement. Because of the element of martyrdom they see in his case, Walker, who lived in their own conspiratorial dream world, was considered a special boon by the extremists. Cries Billy James Hargis in his usual jumble of emotional verbiage: "The purge of General Walker is but an example of the extent to which the Fabian Socialists now in control of our nation will go to extend their program. We now know that it is their intent that all pro-American and anti-Communist material shall be erased from troop information programs, and that all 'right-wing' personnel in the Armed Forces of the United States shall be eliminated to make way for the Fabian Socialists' take-over—aided and abetted by international Communism, its agents and its sympathizers."

14:

In Politics

For the ultraconservatives, the first three years of the 1960s brought some measure of success on the political front. Their triumphs did not match their defeats or greatly ease their frustrations but did encourage them to keep up a tenacious rat-a-tat-tat among themselves, in public meetings, in letters to officeholders, and even in the halls of Congress. Representatives Rousselot and Heistand disclosed their membership in the John Birch Society and worked with some of their colleagues in the big conservative bloc of the Eighty-seventh Congress to influence legislation. Their gains were negative—but nevertheless gains—for the Far Right point of view and were scored principally in helping to block advances in domestic social legislation and in foreign relations.

Beyond that, the Movement bombarded Congress endlessly with choice expressions of its attitude, using every possible beachhead to disseminate its views. Rousselot, a first-term congressman elected from Los Angeles County at the age of thirty-two, inserted in the *Congressional Record* a collection of Birch precepts, including the belief that "de-

198

mocracy is one of the worst of all forms of government" and
that "one of our most immediate objectives is to get the
United States out of the United Nations and the United Nations out of the United States." Representative James B. Utt,
also of California, introduced a bill to "rescind and revoke
membership of the United States in the United Nations and
the specialized agencies thereof...." In a speech he had
proclaimed the United Nations the source of world troubles
and the reason "the power, the honor and the prestige of
America have fallen from their high point of 1945 to an absolute zero today." He asserted that "conversion of our limited republic to an unlimited democracy is a death blow to
our nation." As demanded by the Birch Society, We, The
People!, and other Far Right groups, he sponsored a resolution calling for the abolition of the federal income tax.

At other times, Representative Alger of Texas represented
the National Indignation Convention and Representative
John R. Pillion of New York promoted a resolution calling
on the United States to declare nonmilitary "war" on the
Soviet Union. Conservative Southern Democrats joined the
Right-wing Republicans. Representative Dale Alford of Arkansas sought to aid Billy James Hargis in arranging periodic
meetings between Far Right leaders and sympathetic congressmen. In the Senate Thurmond took up the cause of the
Bircher general Walker, exerting enough influence to force
the long, costly, unproductive investigation of his charges
of a "no-win" policy and Pentagon "muzzling" of military
voices. James O. Eastland of Mississippi, chairman of the
Senate Judiciary Committee, charged in a speech against
ending literacy tests for voters that Chief Justice Warren
"decides for the Communists whenever there is a Supreme
Court decision to be made between them and the security
of the United States." He prepared a "box score" on the Supreme Court Justices that was reprinted and distributed by
several Far Right organizations, some of which claim to see

"Communists" behind efforts to achieve racial integration.

Because the Movement had little luck in attracting Northern Democrats, a prize target in the Far Right's effort to add bipartisan flavor to its campaigns was Senator Dodd of Connecticut. He made frequent appearances as a member of the Schwarz faculty, but beyond that flirted gingerly with the ultraconservatives. He bowed out of a rally of Young Americans for Freedom at Madison Square Garden, where he was to have been presented an award for stanch conservatism and active anticommunism. He said he did not want to be the only Democrat on the program.

The only other Democrat scheduled was General Walker, who was seeking the Texas gubernatorial nomination at the time. His invitation was withdrawn when Senators Goldwater and Tower, the top political favorites of YAF, refused to appear on the same platform with him.

Goldwater and Tower said that as members of the Republican Party they could not give the appearance of endorsing a Democratic candidate. What they apparently really feared was any sort of public identification with the wild-swinging Bircher. As spokesmen for the conservative bloc in Congress, they have been careful not to dilute their influence by close association with the Radical Fringe. Goldwater especially, although the hero of the Radical Rightists as well as of the much larger body of orthodox conservatives, has been cautious. Perhaps it is his ambition for higher office as well as his convictions that dictates his drawing the line. He has drawn it as far to the right as politically possible, excluding only the Birch leadership (Welch) and, in Goldwater's own words, "the idiots that are always attracted to a movement in its beginnings." He has praised other Birchers as "good," "sincere" citizens.

Many Birchers who do not go along with Welch in his most extreme views admire the handsome Senator from Arizona for the stature he has given the Right Wing on

Capitol Hill. They look to him more than anyone else for effective help in Congress. He excites most of them as much as he does the "respectable" conservatives and the voters of the future who beat the drums for him on campus. They are fully satisfied with the views he has been expressing throughout a decade in the Senate: government has become too federalized, taxes too burdensome; citizens should work for a living instead of looking to the welfare state for succor; more power should be given to states and more freedom to the individual; cut spending; talk tough to Khrushchev.

"The real danger to our country in these days of crisis," the Senator wrote in a *Saturday Evening Post* article, "does not come from the right side of the political spectrum, but from a direction more closely aligned with Communist objectives. It does not come from military commanders, like Maj. Gen. Edwin A. Walker, who want to make sure their troops and the American people are informed of the true nature of our enemy, but from forces which would deny such instruction. It does not come from patriotic Americans who wish to remain vigilant to the threat of internal Communism and to socialist trends, but from people who would blunt that vigilance.

"I believe the great threat, the real danger to our nation, to our way of life and to the cause of freedom throughout the world comes from the leftists in our midst who even today counsel a soft attitude toward Communism, both at home and abroad."

Billy James Hargis called it the best expression of his own position he had ever seen. The writers and broadcasters of the Right, including the Extreme Right, are almost unanimously ecstatic about the personable Phoenix merchant. They see him as their first hope since Robert A. Taft for a President who would return "constitutional government." They are impressed not only with his views but also with his personal magnetism. His warmth and charm have endeared him to some of his more liberal colleagues in the Republican hierarchy as well. Conservatives all over the country have become enchanted with the idea that they may be able to get on a bandwagon of a deep-dyed conservative in the 1964 Presidential contest. Goldwater himself has said he does not want the GOP nomination, but none of his followers will settle for that. The extremists add their backslaps to the hundreds of letters a day that pour into the Goldwater office in Washington. They follow the syndicated column that gives the Arizonan a forum in more than 100 newspapers. They turn out to applaud as he hop-skips about the country with seemingly endless energy to fill speaking engagements.

Welch assured his following that Goldwater was "the ablest and best statesman in America . . . and [the fact] that he disagrees with me should not change the John Birch Society's attitude toward him."

But even if Welch and other extremists considered Goldwater an ogre, they would have to support him for President. As a practical matter, they have nowhere else to go.

There was a time when the Far Right hoped that new and more militant leadership had appeared in the person of Walker, but the hope was not long-lived. Close Walker associates wanted him to seek the nomination for congressman-at-large in Texas, but the general decided that only as governor could he make Texas "a bastion against communism." Tower and Thurmond failed to dissuade him from running, and his poor showing ended his political career almost as soon as it had begun. His later adventure in Mississippi made him a hero to the rabid segregationists but an embarrassment to many others on the Far Right.

Thurmond, the man who championed Walker at the Senate hearing, remains a full-fledged hero of the Ultras in his own right and a Senator they regularly come to for aid. Like Goldwater, Thurmond is a general in the Reserve. He won a number of decorations as an infantry officer in World

War II. A tireless spokesman for the extremists' creed of belligerent stand-up-to-communism, the South Carolina Democrat belongs to that group of militant antiliberals who are convinced that President Kennedy was sold a "no-win" policy by Leftists in the government. The rock-jawed Senator's popularity with the Ultras is greatest in the South, where his uncompromising segregationist view is appreciated as much as his extreme conservatism on other issues. He has said that both major parties are too much alike and that a third party is needed. He could be a powerful spokesman for one if the conservative fringe ever coalesced sufficiently to make a third party possible. Hard-working, teetotaling "Strum" carried four states as the Dixiecrat candidate for President in 1948, when he was governor of South Carolina. But there is little indication that the Far Right would be able to organize an effective third party in the forseeable future even if it should decide on such a course.

The newest hero of the Far Right is Tower, Texas' first Republican Senator since Reconstruction. Since taking his seat in the Upper Chamber in 1961, he has rivaled Goldwater in crisscrossing the country for speeches advocating uncompromising conservatism.

While the Eighty-seventh Congress was in session (1961–62), the Far Right made prodigious efforts to take advantage of the strength of the conservative bloc. Letter-writing campaigns piled an imposing amount of mail on congressional desks. The failure of the Ultra Right to end foreign aid, oust the United Nations, blow up Cuba, impeach Warren, or abolish the income tax were not due to lack of effort. The John Birch Society alone claimed to be able to muster a quarter of a million letters on any issue.

Much of this mountain of paper went to the House, where the conservatives were strongest. The most obvious results were the speeches, resolutions, and votes of the Rousselots, Hiestands, Utts, Pillions, Algers, and others. Less obvious was the influence exerted on other congressmen, legislators not convinced of the plausibility of the positions espoused by ultraconservatives but nevertheless impressed by the volume of mail. The proof that they were impressed is seen in the cautious wording of their replies.

The unimpressed simply passed the Radical Right mail along to an appropriate committee for reply. In the large anteroom between the office of Representative Emanuel Celler, chairman of the House Judiciary Committee, and the committee's hearing room, for example, are rows of files. One thick folder labeled *Supreme Court* has retained its bulk since the advent of the Birch Society no matter how conscientiously the secretaries prune and reply. In the office it is called the "Impeach-Warren file." Answers to demands for impeachment cite Article II, Section 4, of the Constitution: "The President, Vice-President and all civil Officers of The United States shall be removed from office on Impeachment for and Conviction of, Treason, Bribery or other High Crimes and Misdemeanors." The replies, saying that since "no evidence of such crimes" has been offered there are no grounds for impeachment, are usually signed by Celler, a liberal Democrat from New York City. A committee aide says that "the signature on the letter is like salt poured into an open wound."

Mail to congressmen often comes in batches, each concentrating on a single issue. "You can tell when a campaign is under way, because opening sentences will be the same and the same sentences in a hundred letters will be underlined," an administrative assistant said. "We used to put them in a 'crackpot file.' We still have that one but now we have another called 'Birch, Etc.'"

One week's mail to a Midwestern congressman included form letters, all bearing the Birch sticker, in opposition to federal aid to education and housing, federal operation of utilities, the purchase of United Nations bonds, and to the establishment of a Department of Urban Affairs. Others opposed financing of medical care for the aged through the Social Security system.

In reinforcing established conservative views, if nothing else, the letter-writing campaigns had an effect in helping to stall some of the Kennedy program. In the 1962 election campaigns, the Far Right set out to strengthen its toehold in Congress. A national poll at the grass-roots level found that 8 per cent of the respondents favored the aims and methods of the Birch Society. In congressional districts where the figure was above this, ultraconservative hopes were high. Rousselot and Hiestand campaigned for re-election on their records, along with two other avowed Birchers, H. L. Richardson, also of Los Angeles County, and Mayor Jack Seale of Amarillo, Texas. Americans for Constitutional Action endorsed them, along with 150 other House and 19 Senatorial candidates. It assigned field men to aid 11 Senate and 35 House candidates in organizing their campaigns, raising funds, and writing speeches.

There was plenty of advice on strategy. Tower told a *Human Events* rally in Washington that the Right Wing "cannot win at the polls by calling everybody who disagrees with us a Communist."

"We can't win by shouting slogans," he said. "You've got to get to work on the block and precinct level.... You can shout till you are blue in the face but you won't really become effective until you send a congressman of your own view to Washington."

At a training session for volunteer campaign workers in Washington, Rousselot told young Republicans to "hit hard" on the anti-Communist issue. Representative Donald C. Bruce of Indiana told them they should make a campaign point of "expansion of the Communist world" under a Democratic administration. Pillion told them the United States faced "political seizure."

The Birch Society, for effectiveness and in line with stated policy, did not campaign for candidates as a national body.

"We don't take a stand on any candidate," said Tom Anderson in a speech to a meeting sponsored by the America, Wake Up Committee at Clayton, Missouri. "Our business is to educate the people politically, make them aware of the qualifications of candidates and put them to work at the grass roots at home."

Birch activity at the "grass roots," frequently disguised under other names than that of the Birch Society, was considerable in some districts. Wisconsin, which had a number of highly vocal chapters in the Second Congressional District, offers an example. The Congressman seeking re-election was a liberal Democrat, Representative Robert W. Kastenmeier, and the Birchers spared no effort to defeat him. He was associated with sponsorship of the so-called Liberal Papers, a collection of manuscripts in which others advocated such things as the admission of Communist China to the United Nations. He was one of six members of the House to vote against an increase in appropriations for the House Committee on Un-American Activities. Under the names of various "Committees" that appeared on campaign literature and in newspaper advertisements, the Birch Society and other Right-wing groups accused him of subversion. Pamphlets included one with *Mr. K* emblazoned in large red letters (with the rest of Kastenmeier's name in small print), asking why he was "trying to bury us." Newspapers were bombarded with Rightist letters to the editor assailing Kastenmeier. Because he favored medical care for the aged financed through Social Security, a political action committee composed of doctors joined in the attack, contributing substantial funds to defeat him.

Another Birch target in Wisconsin was John W. Reynolds, Democratic attorney general opposed in the 1962 gubernatorial contest by a solid conservative, Philip G. Kuehn.

Reynolds charged that his opponent's campaign depended
upon financing by ultraconservative industrialists and Birchers. He sought to make it the Number One issue. Theodore L.
Taylor, dentist who headed Chapter 849 of the Birch Society
in Madison, endorsed Kuehn, a Milwaukee businessman, and
the endorsement was publicly accepted. Taylor had been a
delegate to Wisconsin's Republican convention earlier in the
year.

Despite the efforts of the Far Right, both Reynolds and
Kastenmeier were elected. Whether the highly vocal role of
the relatively small number of Radical Rightists had helped
or hurt their favorites was not clear because other more important issues, such as the positions of the gubernatorial candidates on taxes, clouded analysis. But elsewhere in the country there was plenty of solid evidence that the Far Right
provided shaky rallying ground for anyone aspiring to high
political office. Wherever ultraconservatives campaigned on
Birch principles they lost. November 6, 1962, was a day of
political disaster for those who carried the banner of the Far
Right unflinchingly. Rousselot, Hiestand, Richardson, and
Seale all were defeated, leaving the Birch Society without
avowed membership in Congress. Twelve of the 19 senatorial
candidates endorsed by Americans for Constitutional Action
lost.

Rousselot, fluent young former public relations man, was
stopped by Assemblyman Ronald Brooks Cameron, who
campaigned against "Birchism" and kept referring to his opponent, who later became a Birch official, as a "Bolshevik of
the Right." Hiestand, seeking a sixth term, was defeated by
a Los Angeles city councilman, Everett G. Burkhalter, whose
posters proclaimed *Defeat Communism and Birchism*. Richardson, an anti-Communist lecturer and former advertising
man, lost to Assemblyman George E. Brown, liberal Democrat who campaigned as a "100 per cent Kennedy supporter."
Districts newly gerrymandered by a Democratic-controlled

legislature contributed to the defeats of the Birchers. Each polled more than 50,000 votes, however, an indication of the continuing strength of the Far Right in the Los Angeles area.

In the gubernatorial contest in California, the minority strength of the Far Right was a plague to Richard Nixon's strenuous but futile efforts to return to political office. It posed a dilemma, because to win Nixon needed the votes of both the ultraconservative Republicans and independent Democrats. With great travail, he sought to appeal to both, never with much success.

When Nixon decided to seek the GOP nomination for governor he was well aware of the active, well-rooted, and vocal Far Right element in his state. He had accepted its support in his first race for Congress years earlier when Roy O. Day, back on the political scene in 1962 as Rousselot's campaign manager, had helped put him in office. When officials of the California Republican Assembly, an organization of party functionaries and officeholders, met at Santa Maria in December 1961 to begin planning the campaign, there was ample evidence that the ultraconservative juices were coursing strong. Present in his new role as state candidate, Nixon read the pulse and said in a speech that whatever differences separated Republican from Republican, "they are infinitesimal compared with those separating Republicans and this Democratic administration."

Governor Edmund G. Brown accused his prospective opponent of placing opportunism ahead of principle by refusing to fight the ultraconservatives in the Republican Party. Brown said he hoped that responsible California Republicans would not let Nixon "walk both sides of the street much longer." Nixon, Brown said in a speech, "is not joining in the fight against the ultra-Right Wing, although these extremists are a strong force in our state and in his party. All of this places Richard Nixon in a position where he must choose between principle and opportunism. He has chosen the latter. He has

stepped away from those who are fighting the political primi-
tives, and he apparently wants their money and their support."

The Right-wing question was already wracking some local
GOP organizations in California. Some of Nixon's advisers
were fearful that much money normally available to a Republican candidate in the state was being siphoned off into
Birch and Schwarz operations. Young Republican groups,
notably in Los Angeles, were captured by extremist elements.
Still, after his nomination Nixon would need the votes of in-
dependents and Democrats dissatisfied with Brown's administration. California's registration was Democratic, four
to three. He announced that he would not support candidates
who accepted the backing of the John Birch Society and that
he neither wanted nor would accept help from Birchers.

Neither the liberals nor the Rightists let him leave it at
that. One evening, after a speech to the San Fernando Valley
Chapter of the Los Angeles County Medical Association,
this exchange developed: *Question:* "In the Los Angeles
Times of last Sunday, there was an article which indicated
that you were not supporting John Rousselot and Edgar
Hiestand. Many of their thoughts and their feelings and convictions are similar to many of ours, notwithstanding their
membership in the John Birch Society. I wonder if you would
comment on this and your stand on it."

"As a matter of fact, I have not taken any stand against any
of them as individuals," Nixon replied.

". . . I know that there are a great number of people who
have joined organizations like the John Birch Society, the
Minutemen, a lot of others, who believe that political parties
or the present political institutions are inadequate in providing them a proper forum with which to fight Communism.

"Now, here is the difficulty, looking specifically at the John
Birch Society. I have no quarrel with a society that is anti-
Communist—I have no quarrel with anybody who wants to

take a so-called extreme position. After all, I may be extreme in some of my views, or my neighbor may be extreme in some of his. That's an American right.

"But the quarrel is this—and I speak now as a Republican —I say that no Republican candidate for office should seek, or accept, the support of an organization whose acknowledged leader has said on several occasions that Dwight Eisenhower and Foster Dulles were conscious agents of the Communist conspiracy. . . .

"In my opinion, men who do have good, strong convictions —and both of these men you have mentioned, for example, have, in many respects, fine records insofar as some of these basic economic and political issues we have been talking about are concerned—such individuals should, in their own interest and in the interests of their party, either get the John Birch Society to repudiate the kind of leadership it has or they should get out of the organization."

A week later, the Republican Assembly met in Berkeley to endorse Nixon or Joseph C. Shell, an ultraconservative. Nixon demanded that the resolutions committee formulate a strong anti-Birch stand. "No Republican organization can compromise with the demagoguery and the totalitarian views of Robert Welch," he said.

The Nixon statement rocked the resolutions committee meeting. It became boisterous and bitter. The resolution was watered down by amendments but still failed to satisfy the Right-wingers on the committee. Arguments broke out on the floor as it came to a vote. Just before the tally was made a delegate shouted, "All Communists here are ordered to vote in favor of the resolution."

The resolution passed, 22 to 5. As adopted it lacked two of Nixon's strongest points: that Birch members who were also members of the Assembly quit one or the other, and that membership in the Birch Society under Welch's terms was "incompatible with the principles of the Republican Party."

Even so, it was too strong for some delegates. One stalked from the ballroom declaring, "I hereby resign from the organization." He told the committee he was a Birch Society member and would keep right on being one "until we stop socialism in this country."

As the resolution was read again, one delegate shouted that the GOP was in no position to denounce its friends. Another man was booed down when he charged that the resolution was an insult to his congressman, Rousselot.

Later Nixon expressed disappointment in the watered-down resolution but said he was grateful that the Assembly had endorsed him over Shell as its choice for the GOP gubernatorial nomination.

The Los Angeles Young Republicans censured the former Vice-President for behaving in a manner "not conducive to party unity," but Nixon repeated the charge that Welch was an "irresponsible demagogue." Welch seemed unperturbed. He said that 1962 was a "political year" and "those people who expect us to win by political means look at things differently from those of us who are looking ahead." Welch said that if he were a Californian he would vote for Nixon's opponent in the primary but would support either man against Brown.

Nixon beat Shell by a two-to-one margin. But the political strength of the Rightists had been shown. Nearly half a million California Republicans, 34 per cent of the turnout, voted for Shell, re-emphasizing Nixon's ticklish problem of appealing to both the Far Right and to Democrats in the general election.

Early in the campaign Nixon charged two Democrats with helping to organize the riots against the House Committee on Un-American Activities when it had met in San Francisco in 1960. One of them, John A. O'Connell, candidate for Congress from San Francisco, accused Nixon of "deliberate slander." O'Connell said "the charges are totally un-

true and I suspect Mr. Nixon knows they are untrue." The
other Democrat, Assemblyman Philip Burton, said that "in his
desperation to breathe life into a losing campaign for Governor, Nixon has again resorted to his favorite campaign
tactic of character assassination."

The charges themselves, blurted out in the heat of an argument with Governor Brown, did not suddenly reinject the
communism issue into the campaign. Nixon had done that
almost immediately after winning his party's primary by
excoriating the Democratic governor's administration for
"not having adopted any anti-subversive legislation these
past two years." In addition to planting the soft-on-commu-
nism innuendo, Nixon recalled as a strategist Murray
Chotiner, who was identified in the public mind with charges
of employing smears in previous Nixon campaigns. Nixon,
Brown responded, "is no longer hopeful of winning on legitimate issues if he must reach into his bag of shabby tricks for
the old slander that has been his stock-in-trade for the past
sixteen years."

"My opponent's sudden emphasis on anti-Communism,"
he added, "is nothing more than a sop to the John Birchers
in his own party. . . . He is willing to create this totally false
issue as a come-on to the Birchers even while he tries to
masquerade as a moderate among the most thoughtful elements in his own party."

Nixon was also plagued by the activities of some of his
supporters. Democrats obtained court orders to halt the distribution of three pieces of campaign literature. One, which
came to be known as The Little Red Book, called Brown a
Communist "apologist and appeaser." The red-covered booklet was entitled "California: Dynasty of Communism." It was
written by Karl Prussion, a Right-wing crusader and self-
styled former counterspy for the FBI who publishes a newsletter called Heads Up in Los Altos, near San Francisco. The
Brown camp also made political capital of Right-wing distribution of bumper strips reading "Is Brown a Pink?" and

"Earl Warren Should Be Impeached." Some Republican
leaders came out against Nixon. He lost by nearly 300,000
votes, apparently ending at the age of forty-nine what had
been a spectacular political career. Republican Senator
Thomas Kuchel, who dissociated himself from the Far Right
without equivocation, was re-elected by about 700,000 votes.
Nixon was hurt by his lack of forthrightness and his failure
to convince the electorate that he had really found a Communist menace in the state.

Californians also turned back a Right-wing drive to pass
the so-called Francis Amendment to the state constitution.
The proposition, named for Assemblyman Louis Francis of
San Mateo, who introduced it, would have made it possible
for courts, grand juries, or governmental bodies of various
kinds or any of their officers legally to designate a person or
organization as "Communist" or "subversive." The initiators
collected nearly half a million signatures to qualify this
amazing proposal for the ballot. It was overwhelmingly defeated, but nevertheless drew about a million favorable
votes.

Far Right activity, while strongest in California, also
stirred up a furor in Texas. The Eighteenth Congressional
District, in the High Plains of the Panhandle, offered a lively
example. For years the ranchers and townspeople there had
sent Democrat Walter Rogers to Washington to represent
them. Now the Birch Society was making its presence felt
and had nominated one of its own, Mayor Seale of Amarillo,
as Rogers' Republican opponent.

As in other towns, the secretive Society had fomented
divisiveness and dissension in Amarillo, separating church
congregations, splitting the city government, harassing teachers and librarians, breaking friendships. As in other towns,
the Birch brand of superpatriotism introduced the anonymous post-midnight telephone call as a weapon of vigilan-
tism.

Special targets were the clergymen. In 1961 Brigadier

General William L. (Jerry) Lee, retired Air Force officer and coordinator for the Birch Society, assailed one minister as a Communist sympathizer and charged that the National Council of Churches was infiltrated by Communists. Leading ministers challenged him to produce evidence. Soon they were receiving demands from minorities in their congregations that they renounce the National Council. The ministers refused to budge. Threats to withhold financial support followed. Several families left the Methodist churches and formed a Congregational Methodist Church. Others left the First Christian Church.

The unquiet spread. The Birchers instituted a purge of school and public library books that were allegedly Communist or obscene. Some novels of established rank were among those removed in 1962.

Even the local Girl Scout organization was fodder for Rightist suspicions. The Birchers led a successful battle against a proposal to put the girls under the direction of a regional council, insisting on retention of local control to avoid the possibility of Leftist influence.

Many sectors of community life were split by the introduction of Birch principles. In 1962 a national Right-wing organization called the Association of American Dentists was formed in Amarillo as a home for ultraconservative dentists unhappy with the established American Dental Association. Many Amarillo doctors sympathized with or joined the Birch Society. One said any physician who spoke up against the Society found that his practice suffered.

The Rightists gained control of the city government. Mayor Seale, like other members of the Birch Society suspicious of the growing federal bureaucracy, turned down a federal grant for a sewage-treatment plant.

After Seale was nominated for Congress, the Amarillo *Daily News* endorsed him. It defended the Birch Society as "decent and God-fearing." The city's other paper supported

Rogers. It noted that the town had become so wracked by dissension that high school students were calling their teachers "Communists."

Rogers made Seale's Birch membership a major issue, charging that the Society's tactics fostered hatred. He won handily. Once again the electorate, even in an area where the Radical Rightists had made serious inroads (the Panhandle is Hargis as well as Welch territory), left no doubt about the majority view on Birch principles and methods. Once again the superpatriotic minority proved to be more vocal than sizable. But the wounds it had inflicted on the town could not heal overnight, and while the Society had suffered a sharp rebuke, it did not fold its tents and depart.

There were other battlegrounds around the country. One of the most important to the ultraconservatives furnished one of the worst setbacks. Because of his memorandum on the military and because of his liberal outlook on foreign affairs, the Far Right went all-out to defeat Senator Fulbright in Arkansas. His opponent, Dr. Kenneth Jones, a bone surgeon who took the Birch view that the greatest threat to the nation was internal, was backed by Americans for Constitutional Action, the Harding College team, the Conservative Society of America, and—behind the scenes—members of the Birch Society. Goldwater and Tower spoke for him. Jones termed the campaign a battle between conservatism and communism. Fulbright called him a "fear-stricken radical who blindly refuses to face even the challenges or opportunities of the future." Fulbright won by a margin of more than two to one.

In North Dakota, Senator Milton B. Young, moderate Republican, was threatened with a Rightist purge earlier in 1962. Arch-conservatives considered putting up a candidate against him, a move that might have split the Republican vote sufficiently to elect a Democrat. "Many of them have stated they would rather have a Democrat because it would give them a chance to reorganize the Republican Party, and they can't reorganize it the way they want it—ultra-conservative—as long as they have a guy like me in it," Young said.

Young told the Senate he was "deeply concerned about the increased membership and spreading influence" of the John Birch Society in his state. "It has gained considerable membership in several of the major cities in North Dakota," he said, ". . . and has among its members some of the most able and influential people in each community." Senator Mike Mansfield of Montana interrupted to say "the same thing is happening" in his state.

Young had precipitated the rebellion in North Dakota without realizing it at the time. In 1960 a resolution was offered to the North Dakota state legislature for repeal of the income tax. It was sponsored by the Committee for Economic Freedom and backed by supporters of the John Birch Society, including some people prominent in state politics, farming, and business. The resolution was rejected in the state senate after passing the house. Young helped defeat it by contending that a state petitioning for federal funds for irrigation projects could not demand repeal of the income tax. The letter writers of the Far Right attacked Young vehemently. Support for the Rightists came from the Speaker of the House, R. Fay Brown, from some leaders of the North Dakota Farm Bureau, and from Martin Vaaler, then president of the State Public Service Commission. Vaaler, a Birch Society member, had been one of the sponsors of a Welch trip to North Dakota. Young, commenting on Vaaler's activities, described him as "some kind of a nut." Vaaler retorted: "It is difficult for me to understand why a U.S. senator, sworn to uphold the Constitution, continues to harass patriotic citizens who are aware of the Communist conspiracy and are trying to do something about it."

The Republican Party leadership issued a statement saying it had no tie with the John Birch Society, and the Right Wing eventually decided not to oppose Young. One of the Society's regional coordinators told a Birch meeting in Bismarck that Young had "a good, conservative voting record except on farm policy" and that intraparty squabbling might result in the election of a Democrat. Young was re-elected.

The North Dakota Birchers did not leave the public forum after dropping the Young fight, however. The Bismarck chapters (there are "several" in the town of 27,000, Vaaler said) began a weekly series of "educational" ads in the Bismarck *Tribune*. The first was a reprint of a Westbrook Pegler column crediting the Birch Society with its "first major political coup" in uncovering the Billie Sol Estes scandal in Texas. Pegler said the man originally responsible for exposing the Estes financial manipulations in 1961 was Dr. John Dunn, one of the owners of the Pecos *Independent* in Estes' home town. Dunn says that fighting Estes in Pecos resulted in so much harassment by Estes partisans that twelve members of the Birch Society left town.

The North Dakota story of Birch participation in politics was repeated in other states at all levels of government. "You can't go to a meeting or call a rally," a Midwestern Republican state chairman said, "but what they have ringers in the audience who will ask disruptive questions, provoke heated arguments or even, as they did on several occasions, try to grab the microphone and turn it into a free-for-all."

In Phoenix, the Stay American group put up a slate for municipal office that opposed the city-manager form of government, which the Hard Right views as a Communist device to wrest control of local government from the citizenry. One of the Stay American candidates declared that Reds were preparing to "blow up State capitols at a certain signal." Phoenix voters decided to take their chances and turned down the Stay American candidates. Goldwater had been instrumental in bringing city-manager government to his home town in the first place.

But despite their own shutout at the polls, the Far Right was heartened by 1962 victories of less radical conservatives, many of whom share some of the views of the Fringe. In Louisville, M. G. Snyder welcomed the support of both Americans for Constitutional Action and the Birch Society in his successful campaign to unseat his liberal Democratic opponent, Representative Frank W. Burke. In Colorado, Peter H. Dominick beat another liberal Democrat, John A. Carroll, to gain a Senate seat. His effective and often-repeated ploy was the Right-wing favorite, "I do not question his patriotism, but . . . ," the *but* being followed in this case by such generalizations as "apparently Carroll has been blind to the crucial struggle in which the free world is engaged." In Washington, K. W. Stinson, a conservative Republican, defeated Don Magnuson, Seattle Democrat who had represented the Seventh Congressional District, considered a Democratic stronghold, for a decade. Stinson had been associated with a Puget Sound Anti-Communism School conducted by Schwarz and was endorsed by Americans for Constitutional Action. In the state's senatorial contest, the Reverend Richard G. Christensen, Lutheran minister making his first bid for public office at thirty-two, gave Democratic Senator Warren G. Magnuson a scare by coming within 45,000 votes of an upset. He was aided by the Birch Society, which had a good deal of strength in rural eastern Washington.

In Kansas, ultraconservatives were able to take control of the Republican Central Committee for Sedgwick County (Wichita). In Michigan they retained a key position of power in the Republican organization of the Fourteenth Congressional District in spite of the personal intervention of George Romney. Richard Durant of the Birch Society was re-elected vice-chairman of the organization at the height of Romney's campaign for governor. The district includes wealthy suburbs of Detroit, and the ultraconservative strength there was shown in the election of Durant despite the opposition of the popular governor-to-be and such other Michigan Republican leaders as John Feikens, former state chairman and federal judge; Wilber M. Brucker, former governor and Secretary of the Army; and Charles H. King, former Federal Communications Commissioner. Just before he was re-elected, Durant announced that he had resigned from the Birch Society to meet Romney's objection, but nobody believed he could so suddenly change his convictions. In any case, his re-election to the position of actual power in the Republican unit was an embarrassment to Romney for the rest of his campaign. One week after the "resignation" Durant told the Conservative Club in Dearborn that he had not abandoned his basic philosophy.

Ultraconservative strides in 1962 also put at least a slight flaw in the shiny image of another prospective Republican Presidential candidate. Organization of the Conservative Party in New York, "to give New York's conservatives a vote in statewide elections," resulted in about 140,000 votes for governor on the new Conservative line on the ballot. Most of them would have gone to Nelson Rockefeller, the Republican candidate for governor, had there been no Conservative candidate. The Conservative campaign against Rockefeller thus helped to prevent him from exceeding the margin by which he had won his first term, a goal that would have further enhanced his standing as the leading choice for the presidential nomination in 1964. His plurality of 518,000 was impressive, but 55,000 below the margin he got when he became governor in 1958.

The new party was formed to force a conservative turn in Republican policies and choice of candidates. Both Rockefeller and Senator Javits were regarded by the Right Wing in New York as no more satisfactory than liberal Democrats. The new party set forth this position: "New York's conservatives have no vote in state-wide elections. The reason is simple. Both major parties in the state are now dominated by the liberals. These elements have saddled the Republican Party with the leadership of Nelson Rockefeller, the New Deal's legacy to the GOP, and Jacob Javits, the only 'Republican' with a 100% ADA voting record." The statement, in letters seeking financial aid, called for ending "government support of special privilege," farm controls and subsidies, and favors for industry.

Javits denounced the dissident Republicans as members of the Radical Right. "They are pursuing a course of rule or ruin and are so far outside the spectrum of American political life," he said, "that it is my duty and yours to prevent them from subverting and splitting the Republican party."

The new party plunged ahead, offering candidates for five statewide offices. It formed 140 local clubs in 40 of the state's 62 counties. Its objective was to show enough strength at the polls to demand a voice in the selection of Republican candidates in the future. This it could do, as the Liberal Party has been able to do on the Democratic side, by commanding the loyalty of enough voters to become the balance of power in a close election. Both the Liberal Party, and before it the American Labor Party, have exerted great influence over Democratic policies. In 1962 the Liberals collected about 250,000 votes for Governor Rockefeller's Democratic opponent, Robert M. Morgenthau.

The slimmer Conservative vote was nevertheless impressive enough to inspire the organizers to hold fast and gird for 1964. The party had started from scratch, with candidates for the major offices who were political unknowns—David H. Jaquith, Syracuse steel manufacturer, for governor; Kieran O'Doherty, New York City lawyer, for the Senate. Jaquith polled nearly three times as many votes as needed to put the party on the ballot in future elections. This allows the Conservatives to nominate candidates, or to endorse major party candidates, at state conventions rather than by petition. But while the 2½ per cent of the total vote for governor polled by the Conservatives was a creditable beginning, it was considerably short of the strength the new party would need to accomplish its aims.

Organizers of the Conservative Party included two *National Review* editors, Frank S. Meyer and William F. Rickenbacker, son of Eddie Rickenbacker; Daniel G. Buckley, onetime assistant counsel to McCarthy's Investigations Subcommittee of the Senate Government Operations Committee; novelist Taylor Caldwell; and Mrs. Alfred Kohlberg, widow of the late importer and lobbyist for Chiang Kai-shek. The executive committee included Joseph H. Ball, former Minnesota senator. O'Doherty, endorsed by Americans for Constitutional Action when he ran against Javits, was the first state chairman. He was aided in organizational work by Marvin Liebman, a Right-wing promoter whose public relations office was used by Fred Schwarz to set up his New York School of Anti-Communism.

Jaquith, in his campaign against Rockefeller, openly welcomed the support of the John Birch Society. The Conservative candidates ran on a platform of "victory over communism" and strengthened free enterprise. The platform urged reduced contributions to the United Nations, "elimination" of the Communist regime in Cuba, restrictions on foreign aid, reduced income taxes, and curbs on labor unions. At a fund-raising rally in Madison Square Garden, some of the 8000 Conservatives present held up signs asking: *Jack, why blockade? Invade!* Many shouted "Fight, fight!" whenever speakers attacked the administration's course in dealing with Castro.

But as a political issue, Cuba proved a disappointment to conservatives all along the line. Goldwater charged in a statement the day before the election that Kennedy had committed a grave error in agreeing not to invade Cuba if Soviet missile installations there were dismantled. The Committee for the Preservation of the Monroe Doctrine, headed by Eddie Rickenbacker as chairman, was formed to protest the pledge as a "guarantee" that Cuba would be permitted to remain a Communist nation. But the general public, relieved that Kennedy had been able to force a Russian backdown without war, had little appetite on Election Day for brinksmanship. Some of the conservative stalwarts who had been critical of the President's measured course, including Senator Homer E. Capehart of Indiana and Representative Judd of Minnesota, went down to defeat. Some of the extremists had relied even more heavily than Capehart on the Cuban issue. Rousselot used a big map of Cuba at rallies, pointing out "missile bases" and "army camps" for "Russian, Czech, Red Chinese and Algerian soldiers." He demanded immediate military intervention. In Arkansas, Goldwater, appearing in support of Fulbright's opponent, condemned the chairman of the Senate Foreign Relations Committee for urging caution in dealing with the Castro regime. Dr. Jones sought to depict Fulbright as an instrument of appeasement, a "one-world senator" whose views could lead to a socialistic government. Fulbright responded that the real weaklings were those who demanded immediate victory at any cost. He said it was foolhardy to talk of absolute victory in a world that must live with the constant threat of holocaust, that the alternative to war and destruction was negotiation.

The voting public rejected the extremists, slamming the brakes on much of the momentum the Movement had worked so diligently to generate.

15:

In the Public Forum

The professionals of the Far Right have thrived on the public debate that has swirled about them. They have been able to convince their followers that attacks on them, their philosophy, and their methods are the result of "plots" against them, designed in Moscow and transmitted to the United States for execution by the liberal-socialists. They cite as evidence articles on their activities in the Soviet Army paper, *Red Star; The Worker*, Communist Party weekly; and *The People's World*, published in San Francisco. The conspiracy, they charge, makes it difficult for them to get a fair hearing in the public forum.

Edward Hunter, one of the Far Right's experts on brainwashing, offered an explanation in testimony before the Senate Subcommittee on Internal Security in 1961.

"I have watched an actual grass roots movement against Communism develop all across the U.S.A., and I have noted a new, highly coordinated drive go into high gear to tear this anti-Communist movement up by the roots and destroy it.

223

... It is an organized psychological warfare operation that has all the marks of staff planning.

"A quick Red operation is attempting to push this Administration, the press and the public into a trap that would eliminate the anti-Communist program in the United States. . . .

"The Reds have always demanded that inquiry of any kind into Red manipulation should be forbidden, calling it undemocratic, a reactionary or fascist activity, illegal, unfriendly, hostile. They use the word 'rightist' or 'extreme rightists' as smear words to describe anti-Communism teachings. . . ."

Hargis, reprinting Hunter's words, told his followers: "In the future whenever you read an attack against an anti-Communist leader, you can be sure it was inspired by Moscow."

Conservatives who flinch at being identified with the Far Right frequently respond to attacks on the Right with demands that Liberals look for the extremists in their own house. Goldwater said that even if the extremists of the Right were likened to men throwing rocks at the house of democracy, he feared them less than he did the extreme liberals who were "inside breaking up the furniture." The Americans for Democratic Action, when called the John Birch Society of the Left, responds that it believes in working "within the framework of the law," that comparing the ADA with the Birch Society is like comparing the Mayo Clinic with faith healers.

Time and again the shouts from both wings have prompted moderate voices to rejoin the debate. An editorial in the *Observer, The Wall Street Journal's* Sunday paper, stated:

People who profess to believe, among many other things, that President Eisenhower was some kind of a dupe of the Communists scarcely commend themselves to reasonable men or rational discussion . . . the extreme

Rightists, by calling so much attention to themselves
and drawing such exaggerated attention from so-called
liberals, help to obscure the real dangers of the extreme
left. They have accomplished the self-defeating feat of
making themselves appear, in many eyes, a serious
threat to the nation, whereas the actual threat is the col-
lectivist conspiracy which the United States is supposedly battling all over the world ... whatever one's politics it is a pity to have [the] debate confused in a barrage of extremist and counter-extremist charges.

The Kennedy administration at first sought to discount the
Far Right. "I don't think you fight it," said Lawrence
O'Brien, the President's congressional liaison man. "You just
don't take this type of thing and give it status by making a
frontal attack on it."

The President, however, eventually felt forced to take
public note of the clamor. In Seattle for a centennial program at the University of Washington, he told his audience
of the complexities of the global situation and of the problems inherent in facing them. "These burdens and frustrations," said the President, "are accepted by most Americans
with maturity and understanding. They may long for the
days when war meant charging up San Juan Hill—or when
our isolation was guarded by two oceans ... but they know
that those days are gone—and that gone with them are the
old policies and the old complacencies. Most realize the situation but there are others who cannot bear the burden of a
long twilight struggle. They lack confidence in our long-run
capacity to survive and succeed. Hating Communism, yet
they see Communism in the long run, perhaps, as the wave
of the future ... and they want some quick and easy and
final and cheap solution now."

"There are two groups of these frustrated citizens far
apart in their views yet very much alike in their approach,"

Kennedy continued. "On the one hand there are those who urge upon us what I regard to be the pathway of surrender—appeasing our enemies, compromising our commitments, purchasing peace at any price, disavowing our arms, our friends, our obligations. If their view prevailed the world of free choice would be smaller today."

That was for the ban-the-bomb marchers and those who would disarm unilaterally. Of the Ultras of the Right, the President said: "On the other hand are those who urge upon us what I regard to be the pathway of war: equating negotiations with appeasement and substituting rigidity for firmness. If their view had prevailed we would be at war today, and in more than one place."

Soon afterward in Los Angeles the President repeated his view. Outside the Hollywood Paladium, Right-wingers were picketing in the slight chill of a November evening. Inside, the Kennedy oratory was heated: "In the most critical periods of our nation's history, there have always been those on the fringes of our society who have sought to escape their own responsibility by finding a simple solution, an appealing slogan or a convenient scapegoat... At times these fanatics have achieved a temporary success among those who lack the will or the wisdom to face unpleasant facts or unsolved problems. But in time the basic good sense and stability of the great American consensus has always prevailed.... Under the strains and frustrations imposed by constant tension and harassment, the discordant voices of extremism are once again heard in the land. Men who are unwilling to face up to the danger from without are convinced that the real danger is from within."

Striking at those who pluck at the strings of national emotion, the President continued, "They look suspiciously at their neighbors and their leaders. They call for a man on horseback because they do not trust the people. They find treason in our churches, in our highest court, in our treatment of water. They equate the Democratic Party with the welfare state, the welfare state with Socialism, Socialism with Communism. They object quite rightly to politics intruding on the military—but they are very anxious for the military to engage in their kind of politics.

"So let us not heed these counsels of fear and suspicion. Let us devote less energy to organizing armed bands of civilian guerrillas that are more likely to supply local vigilantes than national vigilance. Let our patriotism be reflected in the creation of confidence in one another, rather than in crusades of suspicion."

In the fall of 1961 Walter Reuther, president of the United Auto Workers Union and a vice-president of the AFL-CIO, discussed the matter with Attorney General Robert Kennedy and promised to write a memorandum for him. That memo, a twenty-four-page blueprint for action against the extremists, was submitted to the Justice Department on December 19, 1961. It had been prepared by Reuther's deputy, his brother Victor, who said in an accompanying note: "We are hopeful that this memo may have some value to you in focusing attention upon possible Administration policies and programs to combat the Radical Right." The Reuther brothers wrote that five areas needed immediate attention:

1. *"The Radical Right inside the armed forces presents an immediate and special problem requiring immediate and special measures."*

Under this heading Reuther recommended that Secretary McNamara investigate the extent of Radical Right influence in the military himself. The memo recalled the Army's refusal to accept a resignation General Walker submitted in 1959 when he charged that a fifth column was working in the American military establishment. It continued: ". . . it also appears to have been widespread pressure from Right Wing generals and admirals in the Pentagon which brought about the recall to duty of General James Van Fleet. It is common knowledge that General Van Fleet has himself been a member of the extreme wing (board member of For America, endorser of the Florida Coalition of Patriotic Societies, board of advisers of H. L. Hunt's Life Lines). . . . All that the recall has accomplished is to embarrass the Administration's ambassador to the United Nations." Van Fleet, Army consultant on guerrilla warfare, blamed Ambassader Adlai E. Stevenson for the U.S. failure to provide air support in the Bay of Pigs invasion and said he would have fired him.

2. *"The Radical Right and the attorney general's subversive list"* was dealt with next.

"The Attorney General's list of subversive organizations is lending aid and comfort to the Radical Right. Although the Radical Right poses a far greater danger to the success of this country in its battle against international Communism than does the domestic Communist movement, the latter has been branded subversive by the government and the former not. . . . The list today is almost like a *Good Housekeeping* seal for the Radical Right . . . [and] *as long as it exists* it should not remain one-sided and permitted to work in favor of the Radical Right."

"It might be advisable," continued the memo, "for the Attorney General to announce at this time that he is going to investigate one or more of these organizations with a view to determining whether charges will be filed and hearings held on the question of listing one or more of these organizations. The mere act of indicating that an investigation will be made will certainly bring home to many people something they have never considered—the subversive character of these organizations and their similarity to listed groups on the Left."

One specific proposal was that FBI agents infiltrate ultra-Right organizations to determine if their actions could be classified as subversive.

3. *"The flow of big money to the Radical Right should be dammed to the extent possible."* The proposal:

"As funds are a source of power to the Radical Right, action to dam up these funds may be the quickest way to turn the tide now running in their favor." The memorandum suggested that tax exemptions be carefully checked, that lists of major donors to the Far Right be made public, and that the Federal Communications Commission check radio and television stations carrying Far Right propaganda but listing their programs as religious, news analysis, or public service. It said that "Know Your Enemy," a five-minute, six-day-a-week radio program on WEAM, Washington, would be a good place to start. The program's commentator had said that "Gus Hall of the Communist Party had a plan for staffing the Kennedy Administration with his followers and that it was already working successfully."

Before the memorandum was submitted, the Internal Revenue Service had begun a review of organizations incorporated as tax-exempt religious or educational groups to determine whether any were dispensing political propaganda.

The memorandum also suggested:

4. *"The administration should take steps to end the Minutemen."*

5. *"The domestic Communist problem should be put in proper perspective for the American people, thus exposing the basic fallacy of the Radical Right."*

In this section Reuther made a point that had long concerned liberals.

". . . The Director of the FBI, Mr. Hoover, even though he made an admirable recent statement concerning the Radical Right, exaggerates the domestic Communist menace at every turn and contributes to the public's frame of mind upon which the Radical Right feeds. Assistant Attorney General J. Walter Yeagley, who continues in charge of internal security matters, has always maximized the domestic Communist menace. There is no need of a further effort to dramatize the Communist issue. The need now is to rein in those who have created the unreasoned fear of the domestic Com-

munist movement in the minds of American people and
slowly to develop a more rational attitude towards the
strength of this movement. Without forbidding dissenting
officials from expressing a contrary viewpoint (and thus
evoking charges of muzzling Hoover, etc.), any effort to take
a more realistic view by leaders of this Administration would
probably cause most of the Administration officials to fall
into line and even some legislators might be affected thereby.
Fifteen years of overstating a problem cannot be reversed
overnight, but thoughtful handling can reduce tensions and
misconceptions in this area too."

In a note accompanying the memorandum, Walter Reuther wrote ". . . this is not a problem that can be swept under
a rug. The Administration can no more combat the Radical
Right by being 'tough on domestic Communism' or appeasing Radical Right generals than the Republican Administration was able to fight McCarthyism by its own excesses in
this area. It is very late in the day to start dealing with these
problems, but it will never get any earlier."

No formal action was taken on the suggestions, although
the document was read by key members of the administration and circulated to sympathetic congressmen. The Defense Department opposed political probes in the armed
services. Calls for a congressional investigation of the activities of the Far Right were rejected.

J. Edgar Hoover, whose book *Masters of Deceit* has been
a favorite of anti-Communists, counseled self-restraint among
Rightists in the weeks after the President's speeches. In 1962
he made his views on the Far Right even clearer. Writing in
the *Journal* of the American Bar Association, the nation's
Number One G-man congratulated the legal group for the
approach it had taken compared with that of the Hargises
and Welches. He said: "Just because the Communists have
no respect for law and order does not mean that we should
retaliate in kind. Cries for legal shortcuts, vigilante methods

and less reliance on legal processes, though based on the most patriotic motives, are most shortsighted.... Emotional outbursts, extravagant name-calling, gross exaggerations hinder our efforts. We must be very careful with our facts and not brand as a Communist any individual whose opinion may be different from our own. Today far too many self-styled experts on Communism are plying the highways of America giving erroneous and distorted information. This causes hysteria, false alarms, misplaced apprehension...."

Hoover praised the Bar Association's efforts to foster "high level, dignified, objective seminars on Communism through the cooperation of local bar associations throughout the country."

At about this time Senator Goldwater, while defending the general membership of the Birch Society, told a joint Washington meeting of the Harvard, Yale, and Princeton clubs:

"Conservatives must beat off the idiots that are always attracted to a movement in its beginnings. The idiots are being drawn toward the conservative movement now just as they were attracted to liberalism in the 1930s. There are always people who will go off on a tangent if they don't think their ideas are being carried out to the letter. I mean any group that goes to extremes. I'm a member of the American Legion and I can remember when it practiced some of the things we object to in the John Birch Society. My chief objection to the John Birch Society is its leader. He is intemperate and unwise. I wish he would step out so the fine, responsible people who are members could take charge."

But tens of thousands still believe in the Far Right gospel and still slip dimes and dollars into envelopes addressed to Robert Welch, Billy James Hargis, and other Far Right organizers. This had been anticipated in the Reuther memorandum: "As the Radical Right cannot be wished away or ignored, likewise its demise is not something that can be readily accomplished. The struggle against the Radical Right is a long-term affair: total victory over the Radical Right is no more possible than total victory over the Communists. What are needed are deliberate Administration policies and programs to contain the Radical Right from further expansion and in the long run reduce it to its historical role of the impotent lunatic fringe."

This was followed by a footnote: "Private agencies can do much to identify and expose the Radical Right. Indeed, in the long run the extent of participation by private agencies in this struggle is more likely to determine its outcome than anything the government can do. The press, TV, church, labor, civic, political and other groups whose constitutional freedom is directly involved must carry the prime burden in this struggle."

But private action to counteract the Extreme Right frequently has been weak. A Hollywood rally in support of the United Nations and free speech found few supporters. One movie star was quoted as saying, "I don't want to get involved in anything more controversial than a charity for crippled children." Some were intimidated by the bombing of the homes of two California ministers who had spoken out. Others who preached good sense from their pulpits, and there were some in every part of the country, were victims of middle-of-the-night telephone threats.

When liberals and liberal organizations did speak up, in print or on the podium, they usually limited themselves to attacking the evils of extremist tactics. They made little effort to slake the obvious thirst of the American public for information about Communists and communism. They continued to leave this important task to Rightists, who filled the vacuum with a distorted picture.

The debate on the philosophy of the ultraconservatives continued, however. Among their most aggressive opponents have been the clergy. The General Council of the United

Presbyterian Church assailed extremist tactics. Methodists were warned by Bishop Everett W. Palmer of Seattle of a "frightening likeness between certain anti-Communist movements now in vogue across America and events which transpired in Germany and Italy prior to the rise of the Nazi and Fascist regimes." The National Catholic Welfare Conference issued an 88-page booklet attacking Right-wing militants for fomenting what it termed "a virulent form of disunity that is dangerously weakening the nation." In the booklet Father John F. Cronin, assistant director of the conference's Social Action Department, said he was "convinced that three-fourths of these extremist groups are making a financial racket of the fight against communism. . . . They're in it for money." The National Council of the Episcopal Church urged Episcopalians to examine the "motivations and methods of those who profit from the business of attacking the churches."

But the profiteers are formidable adversaries. They have had time to lay the groundwork. Their torrent of "documentation" for members and prospective followers continues unremittingly. Much of this flock now "knows" that all criticism of them is part of a plot to soften them up for the Communist takeover. As a woman member of a Chicago chapter of the John Birch Society remarked, "They are really doing a job on us. Some people won't even talk to me any more. They think I'm crazy." She knows she isn't. The newsletters and pamphlets she reads and the tape recordings she hears at the monthly meetings tell her she is right and the "duped" are wrong.

four:
The Future

16:

The Reckoning

Far Right activity has been intense and widespread since 1958. What accounts for its penetration into American homes and communities? Basically its appeal is to the frustrated, the ill-informed, the thoughtless, the insecure, the suspicious, or the bigoted.

In the autumn of 1961 Representative Rousselot inserted in the *Congressional Record* an article by Slobodan M. Draskovich, a member of the National Council of the John Birch Society and editor of *Srpska Borba,* a Serbian nationalist weekly newspaper published in Chicago. This rambling, vitriolic attack on the Liberal Establishment pointed up the frustrations of the Right: "Are the Liberals worried because recent events have filled the American cup of bitter disappointment, humiliation, appeasement, containment, surrender and shame to the brim?" Are they alarmed, Draskovich asked rhetorically, "at the USSR launching a man into space before us," at Laos, at Cuba, at the visit to the United States of the "criminal" Khrushchev, at aid to Tito, and at the United States path "from defeat to defeat"?

Current world crises have indeed engendered doubt and dissatisfaction. Yalta, Potsdam, and Berlin; the U-2; Cuba— these and similar events have given rise to a sense of strain and anxiety throughout the body politic. But only the extremists attribute whatever errors of judgment have been made and whatever situations resist simple solutions to bad faith on the part of government officials, and only they blame the cold-war stalemate on an internal Communist conspiracy. Only the Far Outs impute treasonous intent to the Supreme Court, the Congress, and a wide variety of social, cultural, and religious agencies. Only the Arch Rightists believe that Russian achievements are traceable to American duplicity and connivance; and only they see the solution in substituting for democratic institutions the doctrinaire, totalitarian structure of the Communist Party and the John Birch Society.

Few thoughtful persons would question the fact that Soviet-led world communism constitutes a serious threat to Western democracy. Yet few are frightened enough to succumb to the unbounded suspicions that plague the Radical Right; few are deluded enough to part with reason and embrace the tangled web of paranoia.

"The paranoid personality often gives an impression of self-sufficiency, superiority and certainty," the *American Handbook of Psychiatry* says. "This impression in no way represents the basic internal situation, but only a fixed inability to allow anything to enter which might upset a precarious equilibrium." The handbook also describes the individual who is most vulnerable to paranoia as "a tense, insecure and usually fearful person, one who operates at high levels of anxiety. He usually becomes suspicious and distrustful. He finds it difficult to confide in others and if he does confide . . . he expects to be betrayed."

Few so troubled can put much faith in the administration to combat communism or in the FBI to expose it adequately, particularly when their fears are skillfully exploited by equally anxious demagogues. To the suspicious or naïve, it is sometimes sufficient that a crusader label his efforts "anti-Communist." The possibility that some of his ideas may be dangerous is not investigated.

The frustrations of the Right are as severe on the domestic as on the international front. The Fringe is concerned about high taxes, rising living costs, racial integration, and federal assumption of responsibility for educational, medical, housing, and other needs of the citizens.

Unemployment is a specter for those who fear that a swiftly changing technology will deprive them of job and dignity alike. And moral laxity is a threat to those who do not see how to cope with shifts in social disciplines and changes in traditional values. These are shifts, they fear, that threaten to lead their children from the paths of righteousness and to prevent perpetuation of the established order.

Ultraconservative leaders have had considerable success, simply by preaching anticommunism, in rallying not only religious fundamentalists concerned about heresy but also political, economic, and social fundamentalists concerned about the liberal trends that are threatening their values. Any movement toward racial equality, more effective political democracy, or far-reaching social change is attributed to conspiracy with communism.

Unlike groups that accept the opinions of their opponents as sincere and their actions in the democratic process as honest efforts, the Far Right believes there is no valid opinion except its own. In particular, there are no two ways to fight communism. You either lick the enemy or appease him. Any effort toward accommodation is appeasement, a step toward total defeat. This either-or philosophy includes the tenet that those who reject the "win" choice accept the "defeat" alternative. Thus, ever since the cold war began, every administration has had a "no-win" philosophy.

What the Far Right wants is unchallenged world suprem-

acy and the resulting freedom to return to the relatively un-
complicated life of the nineteenth century. This calls for winning the cold war immediately. Enough of "no-win" delay
and stalemate; attack now. Rickenbacker asks in a Christian
Crusade speech: "Why not now? Are we afraid to fight with
all our powers? Why don't we stamp out the pestilence? Why
not die for a good cause?"

The "win" philosophy, never spelled out but always al-
luded to, apparently boils down to nuclear attack on Communist nations.

"If someone thinks we should have a nuclear war in order
to win," President Kennedy told a 1962 news conference, "I
can inform them that there will not be winners. . . . We have
to proceed with responsibility and with care in an age where
the human race can obliterate itself."

Continued stalemate or mutual concessions, intolerable as
such a fate seems to the Far Right, appeal to the good sense
of the vast majority of Americans more than holocaust. To
responsible citizens not trapped by the either-or choice of
the extremists, existence is not synonymous with appeasement. As Under Secretary of State George W. Ball has
pointed out, "the conduct of foreign affairs today is an in-
tricate, subtle, changing and always uncertain task."

The Far Right applies its either-or philosophy with equal
force to domestic affairs. Any person, church, school, governmental department, or program that is not "free enterprise"
of the Birch brand is liberal, therefore socialistic, therefore
communistic and treasonous. This, the Radicals say, is the
real root of the nation's troubles with communism—subversion right here at home. In the past, such outcroppings have
been rejected, after a good airing, by prevailing common
sense. The untenable positions of the current Rightist Movement have been repeatedly exposed. But there is no denying
that the baffled, the ill-informed, and the immature—in large
numbers—have provided a fertile field for the hysteria, sus-

picion, and disunity being sown in the name of anticommunism.

This Rightist-fundamentalist audience is scattered throughout the country but, except for a few pockets on the coasts,
is heaviest in the South and Midwest. It includes few Negroes and Jews. Nor has there been any great surge of farm
or labor support. The vocal mainstay has been business and
conservative professional people in small towns and suburbs.
This is not to say that the nation's business community is Far
Right. Liberals have been too often guilty of lumping all
conservatives with the small group of arch-reactionaries
among businessmen. Yet the responsible elements of the business community have not spoken out sufficiently to make it
perfectly clear that they feel the line of demarcation between a free enterprise system and Birch-type nihilism is
pronounced and that the businessmen who put up so much
money for the cause of the Far Right are a small minority.

Meanwhile, the professional and commercial anti-Communists have managed to convince the gullible that they should
use Communist tactics against fellow Americans to prevent
the spread of imagined subversion in schools and treason in
government. They have persuaded the confused and thoughtless that some religious denominations are riddled with Communist pastors, and that such institutions as Brotherhood
Week and the United Nations Children's Fund are suspect.
Racial integration means mongrelization. Watch those who
write about or touch upon current facts and problems in
textbooks. The result of all this demagoguery is neighborhood fear and suspicion. The Movement, which seeks to appeal to Christian morality, is markedly un-Christian.

The damage done locally by this mischief should not be
underestimated. This is especially true in the smaller communities. Organized pressure to intimidate teachers, ministers, librarians, editors, and others has had some success,
especially in small towns where leading citizens join Rad-

ical Right groups and condone such methods as anonymous 2 A.M. telephone calls.

In time, the President said in Los Angeles, "the basic good sense and stability of the great American consensus has always prevailed." Meanwhile, the purveyors of fear have found a following and continue to spread their divisive influence.

How long will their rantings find even limited acceptance? Unless there are further upheavals of the magnitude of Cuba, it may not be long. Conservatives who speak for the Reasonable Right, which will always be a force in the democratic system, have taken strong steps to scuttle the Radicals. Robert Welch's wild charges have repelled many who first acclaimed his desire to alert the nation to the Communist menace. Reasonable conservatives are well aware that the nation faces real problems that must be met realistically and that there is no place for misrepresentation in an authentic anti-Communist effort.

Thus William F. Buckley notes that Welch continued to hold such views as that former President Eisenhower was a Communist agent long after the nation had recoiled at the absurdity of the charge. Buckley also tears apart such Welchian extravagances as the view that the Cuban invasion fiasco of 1961 was engineered by the United States government in league with Fidel Castro in order to solidify Communist power in Havana. Buckley, Russell Kirk, Barry Goldwater, and other conservative voices respected by the Regular Right have sought to condemn Welch to ignominy as a man whose judgment is so sadly flawed that he has become a hazard to the Conservative movement. More and more Conservatives once devoted simultaneously to Goldwater, Buckley, and Welch have found it necessary to make a choice. The thoughtful among them are going over the Welchian intemperances more carefully now that spokesmen in their own camp have labeled them for what they are.

When decent, industrious businessmen and others of intelligence realize that they, having aligned themselves with crackpots, are the real dupes, the result is likely to be desertion of Welch by all but the confirmed extremists. Solid conservatism will be stronger as a national force as a result of dissociation from extremism.

What of Rightists, whether followers of Welch, Hargis, or others, who do little independent thinking? Their reeducation will take longer. Those who follow blindly are ignorant of the facts about communism, yet less accessible than others to rebuttal. But strong efforts are under way to reach them by important organizations alarmed at the headway the Far Right has made. The efforts of the Catholic Church are important because of the original success the Birch Society had among Catholics. The booklet issued by the National Catholic Welfare Conference, central administrative unit of the country's Catholic bishops, was for use in sermons, parish study clubs, parochial schools, and church publications in all dioceses. The author, Father Cronin, long-time expert on communism, called its publication the beginning of "a campaign for sanity" in meeting Communist threats. The basic threat is external, not internal, the booklet points out, and extremists are misdirecting their energies by concentrating on "problems that were mostly solved by 1950."

Father Cronin says hysteria and suspicion are becoming increasingly evident in many parts of the country as a result of extremists' identifying "whatever ideas they happen to dislike" with communism.

"When every discussion with the Communist powers is considered a sign of weakness or even treason," the booklet says, "then we are left with only two stark alternatives: surrender or war. Surely our common sense should tell us that we should seek some middle course between these extremes.

"A mature and strong people has the inner strength to

live with occasional frustration and failure. It does not cry disloyalty every time its will is thwarted. When honest mistakes of judgment are made, it seeks to correct them through the democratic process. Temper tantrums resulting from frustrations are not welcomed even in young children. In adults, they are signs of serious immaturity."

An appeal to common sense also has been made on a wide scale in most Protestant churches, in the seminars of the American Bar Association, and in the press.

Delineation of the Communist threat for the edification of the general public is no longer being left entirely to the Far Right, with the result that gradually information is replacing fear and hate. Discourse with the nondemocrats will continue as long as there is a Lunatic Fringe. It occurs in an arena in which every individual and institution appalled by the Fringe can take up arms in defense of the open society. This is the arena of exposure and communication, where good sense usually prevails and bad sense is kept at bay. The open-air atmosphere of this arena would stifle the destructive philosophy of the Far Right whether Goldwater and Company had ever repudiated it or not.

Even the military support the extremists have enjoyed has largely evaporated except among some retired officers of high rank. It slackened markedly after the chackdown on Walker. Without prescribing a strait jacket, the Kennedy administration has reaffirmed and toughened the nation's traditional civilian control of the military. Improved troop and officer education will eliminate doubt about how far to go in expressing political convictions. Officers have been forcefully reminded that they are never off duty so far as public criticism of democratically established national policies is concerned.

Jealousies within the Radical Right may further vitiate the Movement. Suspicious leaders of the chronically disorganized Far Right never have found it possible to work together effectively. And the fulcrum of the Extreme Right, the John Birch Society, has become the butt of a tide of jokes that tend to lump its adherents together as clowns or bigots.

The folk-singing Chad Mitchell Trio's "John Birch Society," a record at first banned as too controversial by CBS, ABC, and all Los Angeles AM stations, neatly summed up the jibes in these lyrics:

Do you want Justice Warren to be your commissar?
Do you want Nina Khrushchev in there with the DAR?
You cannot trust your neighbor or even next of kin.
If Mommy is a Commie then you gotta turn her in.

But the Far Right, though it has been dragged into the glare of merciless publicity, is determined to try to carry on despite the handicap. All criticism is dismissed as Communist-inspired persecution. Welch has built a tight, sturdy organization. Hargis has a dedicated following in the Bible Belt. The crowds attracted to the Schwarz spectacles, although increasingly sprinkled with the merely curious, continue to hold up in centers of conservatism. None of the leaders who have gained power, position, attention, and income are likely to slip back into anonymity without a struggle. The extremists still exercise political influence in some states and localities. And in these years of cold war and racial tensions there could be plenty of frustrations ahead for the Far Right to feed on.

Negro militancy and growing government enforcement of civil rights will test white tolerance even outside the Deep South. Religious rivalries between the fundamentalists and liberals show no signs of abating and are likely to sharpen. Frustrations abroad also are bound to continue. The frightened may reel again under Russian scientific achievements and saber-rattling. This decade may produce rumblings of new perils from Communist China. Another shock of the magnitude of the Communist build-up in Cuba could cause a surge of angry despair and temporary gains in financing and membership of the Radical Right. If United States influence in the United Nations wanes with the increased number and authority of new nations, the Far Right will have paroxysms. Setbacks in brush wars will be charged to treason, and so will summitry and foreign aid.

If the John Birch Society had the power to make its policies those of the nation, it would be more effectively subversive than the Communist Party, because the United States soon would be strangled both economically and politically and would indeed be ripe for Communist takeover. But the Far Right is destined eventually to founder, as the Far Left has, on the rock of reason and public discourse. There are no indications that any totalitarian formula will attract any lasting support in this country; the stabilizing political center is far too strong to yield to nondemocratic influences. Ultraconservatism is a ripple to be reckoned with but is not a wave of the future. Self-government is here to stay. So are taxes. So is discourse. With or without the approval of the Far Right, true patriotism and American resourcefulness probably will continue to keep the Communist menace from making any effective headway in the United States.

Index

About the Authors

Donald Janson and Bernard Eismann are newspaper and broadcast journalists respectively whose careers have been devoted to reporting and interpreting all that is significant in the news. Born in Barry County, Michigan, in 1921, Don Janson graduated from the University of Missouri in 1943, received an M.A. from the University of Minnesota in 1948, and attended Harvard University in 1952 and 1953 on a Nieman Fellowship. Since 1948 he has worked for the *Milwaukee Journal,* the *St. Louis Post-Dispatch,* and (since 1955) *The New York Times.* He is now a *Times* Midwest correspondent. With his wife, Jane, he lives in Chicago.

Bernard Eismann was born in New York City in 1933, received his Bachelor of Arts degree from New York University in 1953 and an M.A. in Political Science from Columbia University in 1959 while on a CBS fellowship. In 1955 CBS News sent him to the Middle East where, as special correspondent, he covered the Arab-Israeli dispute until 1957. In 1959 he was made Staff Correspondent and assigned to Chicago to open a Midwest bureau for CBS News. Roaming the area from Pennsylvania to Montana, Mr. Eismann reports on everything from Chicago crime to space science and is seen and heard on CBS News programs. In addition he is heard twice a week on two radio programs, "Bernard Eismann with the News" and "Observations, USA." In 1956 he married Suzanne Gerber, and with his wife and two children he lives in Chicago.